SHANGHAI YEAR

SHANGHI YEAR

by

PETER BRIGG

WILDSIDE PRESS

**For Susan, my wife, and Bill Dobson, my friend,
who helped me to get to Shanghai.**

Copyright © 1987 by Peter Brigg.

ISBN 0-930261-89-5

SHANGHAI YEAR

This edition published in 2006 by Wildside Press, LLC.
www.wildsidepress.com

MORE WILDSIDE CLASSICS

CONTENTS

SHANGHAI
YEAR
A Westerner's Life in the New China

Introduction

1985 was a particularly exciting and fascinating moment to take snapshots of modern Shanghai, a city which defies any simple summing up but contains, in its blend of China and the West, the clearest signs of the winds of change which are beginning to touch the world's most populous country. This little book will be "snapshots,"—scenes, sketches, moments—of Shanghai now with speculations on their meaning in the atmosphere of China, 1985.

I think myself both qualified and unqualified to write this book. I claim for my qualifications the fact that I am resident here for a year as a "foreign expert" and not many Westerners are that. Moreover, I am teaching at the Shanghai Institute of International Economic Management where my alert and intelligent students have been improving their oral English by engaging with me in discussions of contemporary Shanghai and its place in China. This is a very good time to be in China for it is easy to have Chinese friends and to talk to them about the exciting state of affairs as this vast country "opens" to the West and undergoes yet another shift in its political odyssey towards modernity.

I hope that I can also claim to have a reasonably sharp eye for the sights and moments which represent the many faces of Shanghai. I leave that for my readers to judge.

If I am unqualified to write what follows it is because I am a true "observer" of Shanghai. I speak and understand only the slightest touch of Chinese so I can only watch, not listen. Nor have I experienced this city before August, 1984.

My previous knowledge of China is several months of reading in Canada and, before that, a long friendship with a great scholar of classical Chinese, the late Professor W.A.C.H. Dobson of the Universities of Oxford and Toronto. I was never Bill Dobson's student but for over fourteen years he was my academic father in art and awoke in me a deep interest in the Middle Kingdom, whose language, culture and history were his greatest loves. One theme of this little book is that the new China is in many ways the old China, and I owe my sense of that continuity to Bill Dobson.

Life in Shanghai is full of stunning contrasts to life in the West and it is easy to assume the superior and even arrogant stance that so often marks the view from the developed world toward the Third World. I hope that my snapshots will capture something of the energy, spirit and enthusiasm which really identifies the life of Shanghai, which makes this in many ways the most exciting and fascinating city to live in and to watch. Everything is happening here from computers to street vendors, from violence to the most subtle network of human social contacts I have ever experienced. I hope that some fragments of the experience can be captured here for you, my readers, to enjoy.

P.B.
Shanghai, 1985
Guelph, 1986

Street Scenes

The people of Shanghai live on their streets, whether in the easy public life of the crowded, rambling old residential alleys or the press of the Nanjing Lu (lu is avenue, pronounced loo) and the Huai Hai Lu—surely the world's most crowded shopping thoroughfares. A man neatly attaches a fresh eel to a ten-foot bamboo pole, one end of which rests on a bamboo rack six feet above his head and then, holding the pole carefully in one hand, gently reaches for a forked pole with which he raises eel and pole to the rack above him. On that rack and thousands of others about the city hang dried meat, freshly killed chickens and laundry which precisely proclaims the wearer's identity and taste. On each floor of the two- and three-story shambling old buildings, from nearly every window in the tiny apartments sub-divided from the old mansion houses of the former French and International Concessions, and from every balcony of the waves of new six-story apartment buildings proliferating at a furious pace in the vast new residential districts project the racks with their poles resting on them.

In the streets are people. One cannot imagine how many people. In summer they sit on reclining chairs in the late afternoons and evenings and even sleep out to overcome the stifling heat of the tiny rooms. Old men play cards on low tables, surrounded by packs of eager observers. Any small accident or argument draws instant crowds numbering in the hundreds. Children play on the sidewalks but not in the streets which are a continuing moving maze of bicycles, trucks and cars setting up a din of bells, horns and the slap-

3

ping on the sides of vehicles accompanied by the shouts that drivers use to clear paths. At major intersections not even the traffic policeman can prevent the human wave from stopping buses and trucks as it jaywalks.

In winter the children have a characteristic rounded shape that signifies "layers," veritable mountains of sweaters, shirts and underwears to keep them from the cold indoors and out, for only foreigners heat their rooms in this city of freezing temperatures which has been designated "south" China as it lies south, albeit only 15 kilometers south, of the Yangtze. The round children, arms sticking straight out, bounce as they play. Our Emma, 4, looks the same in winter covered in underwear, tights, pants, spare socks, mittens, undershirt, two sweaters, hat and parka hood as she waddles off to kindergarten where teachers still complain that she is underdressed for the winter-damp concrete rooms of the school. Meanwhile street life goes on for the vast army of vendors selling mandarin oranges, socks, belts, gloves, jeans, chopping blocks, fish, shrimp, charcoal, onions, eggs, pots, pans, peanuts, radish and cabbage cakes fried in oil over charcoal, flatbreads and, in summer, all manner of fresh vegetables. In winter the vendors are bundled in as many layers as the children and they somehow maintain a lightheartedness and energy. Tailors operate on the street, with cutters passing fabric to edge stitchers to finishers whose footpowered sewing machines clank and click and produce "custom" tailoring. Our pants cost $2.00 and never did Levi cords fit so well.

The street tailors are part of the new Shanghai brought about by China's economic reforms. Along with many of the vegetable sellers, shoe repairmen, jeans salesmen, keymakers (a vast industry in a city of several million bicycles each with a lock or locks for which keys can be lost), sellers of ties and socks, the tailors have been stimulated by the new economic freedoms and they are making a killing while the going is good. For although the government has said that its new policies are forever, the people of Shanghai have heard that song

4

before and the vendors themselves, when questioned, agree with my students and Chinese friends that the reforms are putting great stress on the society. The street marketeers are thus the subjects of both envy and derision. Everyone knows that the best of them are making up to Y10,000 per year (the Y, yuan, or "kwai" as it is called ["kwai" means piece] is worth about $.35 at the time of writing) compared to an average city wage of Y780, and that earnings like that are simply fantastic in a society which has controlled incomes quite strictly for many years. Moreover, in a socialist society almost everyone in the cities works as part of a state enterprise so there are no income taxes at all, the state simply pays lower wages. The new entrepreneurs pay no such cut out of their wages and so, like the foreign experts, they pay no taxes whatsoever. For both Chinese entrepreneurs and foreigners there is a theoretical income tax of 15% on income of over Y1000 per month but that figure is virtually impossible for any Chinese and very unlikely for any foreigner. But the suspicion is about that the new street free enterprise cannot last, that there will be a reckoning when all of this activity will suddenly become illegal again and the street sellers or makers will be put out of business or strictly controlled. Combined with the fact that there is still a vague feeling that it is wrong to earn so much money this element of danger keeps many people from going to the streets themselves.

Some do, however, like an English teacher met on the streets selling shirts. He had quit his teaching work, in so doing cutting himself off from the security of his danwei or unit, and was making that high income. Where almost all of his street colleagues know only "Hello," repeating it over and over like so many licensed parrots in hopes of getting attention, this man could actually deal with foreign customers. Yet recently this avenue of career change has been blocked. A City Bureau of Education ruling has come out that teachers cannot quit their jobs. The shortage in this area is acute, the pay and housing conditions provided for teachers are

5

particularly poor, so too many teachers were abandoning their careers for the free markets. For teachers the lure of kwai was proving greater than their devotion to the job they had been trained for by the system and suddenly the rules of a competitive society are playing havoc with state planning. This situation, with the authorities' reaction of creating an emergency rule, is typical of the current unnerving flux of policy as China changes, and it means that one schoolteacher is now free to sell shirts, for the present at least, while others cannot make the same change, for the present at least.

But if some of the street people fear for their newfound profits, others go on as they have for many years. One of my favorites is the rice popper, whom my 12-year-old son Mike or I frequent every second Sunday or so. At her spot (in fact she has many spots in our district) near our building she sets up her strange apparatus on its wheeled cart. It looks like some medieval small arm, perhaps used for sieges of small buildings. Covered in soot and rust is an egg-shaped cylinder about eighteen inches long which can be opened at one end by inserting a one-foot iron rod to use as a twist lever. On the other end is a pressure gauge and surrounding it a circular cage from which protrudes a handle for turning the cylinder when it rests on its side, spit-like, over the flame from a tiny coal-charcoal brazier mounted on the wagon. The cylinder is filled with two cups of rice and several tiny sugar pellets, is sealed and turned slowly over the heat as the pressure builds up inside of it. After about fifteen minutes during which the ancient lady operating this mystic device occasionally leans forward from her stool to stoke the fire or add some charcoal but otherwise concerns herself with revolving the cylinder with one hand while with the other she pumps an old-fashioned fire bellows to enrich the heat, the cylinder is lifted from the heat and aimed down a chute into a large tin box appended to the front of the wagon. The box, which is capped with a wire mesh dome and open only at the receiving end, slides out when full to be emptied into the customer's bag or tin. And what does all of this produce? When the cylinder is opened there is a loud pop and a cloud of smoke and out comes rice crispies, or their Chinese near-equivalent. One pound of rice expands in this manner to fill most of a large green garbage bag (brought from Canada and a curiosity in China) and provides the foreigners with three weeks of breakfasts in Shanghai. It takes about five cylinder loads to convert this much rice and the Chinese find the order amazing. Our Chinese friends find our use for it even more surprising, for the sweetened popped rice is eaten as a treat like popcorn in China but not as a regular food. The popper will also perform her explosive ritual for shrimp slices, fluffing them into shrimp chips, and for certain kinds of poppable nuts. The fee: about 10¢ a pop.

From the street vendors it is an imperceptible hop to the shops, restaurants and larger stores of the city. Many of the smaller shops are open at the front with displays of market goods spilling out into the streets. Everything is crowded and there is a constant struggle to get salespeople to pay attention, although foreigners seem to have an easier time of this even when they are reduced to pointing. And foreigners never seem to have problems with the price or the currency. If in doubt, and the Shanghai dialect makes even those of us who know our numbers unsure of quoted prices, just hand over a bundle of money and the required amount will be taken and the rest politely handed back.

Little misunderstandings will occur, of course. At the small department store in our local market in An Shan there is some nice dark green corduroy. I want to get a jacket made up by the street tailor so I peddle over to buy it. The confusion here is that I buy 8 meters instead of eight che (8 che would be about 3 meters) and I watch in amazement as this enormous piece, large enough to make a small boat sail, is cut and folded and folded and folded into a vast package. I pay, unable to explain the problem (and the piece has been cut, after all) and aware that even this much is very cheap. My

7

wife is horrified. A jacket gets made but the rest of the vast piece has to be shipped back to Canada in our crate. It ends up, one year later, covering a four-seater couch.

Our adventures in stores and restaurants are often highlighted by the humor of mischosen English terms or brand names which suffer horribly from the vast cultural gulf between East and West. Nothing reminds us more that language is based on culture than the discovery of Long March brand luggage, which makes Western feet ache at the very thought while it undoubtedly stands for endurance to the company which makes it. Even more excruciating are Red Flag sanitary napkins and Front Gate gentleman's underwear. White Elephant brand batteries powered our flashlights and radios, although all but the alkaline top of the line lived up to the meaning which we give to the term and had to be bought in twenty-battery lots. There are Golden Cock alarm clocks and, although I did not see these myself, there are apparently Great Leap Forward Floor Polish and Junk socks, the latter bearing a picturesque Chinese boat on the label. After these errors in reference, which are of course cultural rather than linguistic, comes the pleasant and lyrical relief of that author's dream and delight; Flying Fish Typewriters.

But it is in the restaurant where the true problems of translation and transliteration come to the fore. British visitors undoubtedly steer clear of the mysterious dish containing electronic equipment, Chicken Galantine in *Telly*, but the optional preparations for the poor bird as offered on the Jin Jiang Hotel's menu are Roiled Chicken and Asparagus, Chicken Carry a la Indienne and Cream of Chicken "Mother Teresa." After the chicken entree one can look forward to Freshly Rrewed Coffee, if one is willing to risk it. At the Jin Jiang, it should be added, there is very good western cooking and coffee, both far superior to the quality of work offered by the menu writer. But it was there where an aged headwaiter, still proud of the French he had learned before the Revolution, horribly mistook my son's request for red jello and gallantly produced a large dish of maraschino cherries swimming in syrup. Our overwhelming embarrassment at what he obviously considered catering successfully to a very unusual request was answered when I took spoon in hand after he had left the table and downed the intensely sweet concoction, satisfying a secret desire to some day eat such a dish. The horror of those at the table at my indulgence was replaced by the relief of Mike's being able to display the empty dish when the old gentleman returned to see. I swiftly turned to three cups of black coffee, telling my stomach to imagine I had had the sugar before the coffee.

At the Peace Hotel, the other chief Western eating place in the city, it is the Chinese side of the menu which waxes lyrical and occasionally slightly dangerous. Given the Chinese taste for eating many different creatures, although Shanghai people swear that it is only in South China that the adage "If it has four legs and is not a table we will eat it" applies, there is more than a slight sense of adventure in Sauté Assorted Flesh in Bean Paste. The modesty of the chef may be at work in the appelation Sliced Pork and Black Fungus Soup (Homely Dish) but there is a far firmer assertion in the offer of Sauté Hotchpotch (Blessing the Whole Family). Finding just the right descriptive word is also undoubtedly a problem and sometimes success itself in terms of accuracy can carry with it just slightly "off" connotations, as in Wrinkled Skin of Pork (an aged pig?) or Fried Tile Shaped Fish with Sweet Sour Sauce. There were also two daily specials in season at the Peace which caught my attention: Liquor-saturated Crab and Large Fish-head in Casserole Taste Very Good. I did not try the fish head but I'm sure Chinese guests at the hotel did, for whenever we ate fish with Chinese friends we were always offered the head, a great delicacy, and after we always declined there was usually a polite but rapid discussion over who would get it. In any event, after dinner at the Peace, you could nip around to one of the local corner stores with their abundant supplies of candies (Shanghai may well have the world's record in sweet teeth, yet these teeth somehow stay wonderfully white—perhaps it is the notorious quality of dentistry) and try, if you find any, "Fruif Candy & Gum Drips."

Aside from the parrot-like "hello" and the frequent "May I practice English with you?" the most frequent conversational opener for the foreigner in Shanghai is a whispered or low-voiced "Change your money?" China operates on a dual currency system with one type of money, renminbi or peoples' money, for everyone except foreign visitors who have wai wei, or foreigner's money. The foreigner may use renminbi wherever the Chinese do (indeed, he is certain to get renminbi change in the markets or Chinese shops) but only wai wei may be used in foreigner's hotels and Friendship Stores, the special shops set up for visitors in which there is a wide range of goods and relatively little crowding. The popularity of wai wei and the resulting black market in currency arises from the fact that only wai wei can be used to buy most imported goods. In 1985 the exchange rate in Shanghai ran from 1.5 to 1.7 to 1 while the official rate is pegged at 1 to 1.

One result of all this was a good deal of dealing and bargaining by foreigners who knew what was going on. Foreign experts are usually paid in a mixture of renminbi and wai wei. We were getting 30% wai wei, for example. If you did not need to buy too many imported goods, such as familiar cigarettes or Scotch whiskey (the Chinese "scotch" is perhaps the most wicked tasting alcoholic drink I have ever touched), there was a strong temptation to increase your salary by "street converting" your wai wei to renminbi, a shady venture involving you and the moneychanger in a walk around several blocks while you counted his offering and then he counted yours.

Now this procedure is illegal, for in theory Chinese citizens have no rights to be in possession of wai wei and foreigners are supposed to trade at the Bank of China or the exchange desks of the hotels. But this can't work in practice because, for one thing, it leaks all over the place in the course of normal commerce. Every foreigner who pays a market tailor in wai wei is doing something he may legally do, and when the transaction is complete, voilà, a Chinese citizen is holding some of the forbidden currency. Only the wildest reaches of the bureaucratic imagination could hope that the tailor, or taxi driver, or cabbage seller would then rush to the Bank of China and turn in the wai wei at 1 for 1 rather than resell it at 1.7 to 1 or keep it in order to buy quality electronic goods or other black market goods which flow freely into south China and then migrate north to Shanghai. Or he could simply go to one of the many public stores in Shanghai which display wai wei imported goods for purchase by universities or businesses which have foreign currency allocations or by foreigners shopping outside of the Friendship Stores.

So attention focuses instead on the money changers themselves, who in the year we spent in Shanghai became increasingly bold until one propositioned me in the very lobby of the Bank of China. Eventually there was a sweep by police and they disappeared, only to reappear two or three months later to tell my Chinese-speaking foreign friends, one or two of whom actually dealt with them, that they had been sent away but everything was O.K. now. It may have helped that they seemed to be largely members of one of the national minority groups who have special status under the Chinese Constitution (they are, for example, exempt from the birth control laws) and that they were therefore less likely to feel the hand of the law. Or it may have been, as we speculated when they were blatantly operating around the Peace Hotel and the Bank of China, that they had friends in the police who had just received nice gifts from "unknown" sources.

I asked my students about the moneychangers and it opened up one of the most fascinating aspects of Chinese life at the moment. To my surprise my students could not agree on whether the trading was illegal, and even an international law teacher who was one of our English students was uncertain. Law and policy are interlocked in a complicated fashion in China, so that a decree which is not law may define an offense and then again, it may not. When Beijing announces a policy some regions of the country may treat it as absolute while others, such as the proudly independent industrial giant which is Shanghai, may not apply it at all in practice. One is reminded of President Nixon's 55 mph speed limit during the oil crisis of the early 1970's. As a Canadian visitor to Montana, I was told that that state's response to what was perceived as none of the President's business had been to enforce the law with a $10 fine for 56 mph and the same $10 fine for 120 mph!

In China this mixture of policy and law seems to produce a good deal of uncertainty and some confusion, particularly in matters related to economics. The climate for the money-changers could change from week to week in Shanghai, apparently in relation to whether they were perceived as being bad for the city's image or were too active and interfering seriously with visitors. We also heard that the real objection to their practices came from the countryside, for the whole pattern involved their selling foreign goods for high prices to peasants, converting those funds to wai wei in Shanghai and going south to buy more foreign goods and repeat the cycle. This would certainly have accounted for the large amounts of currency that they had to change and it would follow that they were being pressured by the authorities not for changing money, which act seems to fall in the gray limbo of being partly illegal, but because the exorbitant prices they charged the peasants for the goods reached a point of gross excess. In trying to figure out why things happen in Shanghai it is wise to remember the influence on the national policies of the country of the 700 million Chinese living in the countryside. In the case of the moneychangers their real crime may have been extortion in the countryside rather than the changing of funds on the streets of Shanghai.

Whatever their situation of the moment it was clear that the potential spoils of the trade made the changers reckless. In one amazing incident on the Nanjing Lu less than a block from the Peace Hotel (which is at the end of the street where it meets the river, the famous Bund or foreigner's port) I saw about eight of the changers, including a young man with a baby and his wife, get involved in a scuffle over this prime territory within twenty feet of a policeman directing traffic. As the police attitude toward street fighting is to throw every-one concerned into the wagon and sort it out later (it being frankly impossible to sort it out in the shouting mob which forms instantly), it was clear that changing money in a good spot was worth a great risk indeed.

The occasions when one sees people fight in the streets in Shanghai serve as reminders of two things. In a city which lives at such close quarters, domestic lives will inevitably spill out into the streets; dirty laundry will get washed in public. Secondly, the outbursts one does see are really re-minders of the amazing tolerance in a city so crowded and busy that there are many situations which could lead to con-flict. Yet there is pressure on people in the city, a pressure accentuated by the extremes of crowding which occasionally breaks the surface. It certainly leads a watcher to consider what the power of the people must really be like in times of anger or disruption, such as the Cultural Revolution, even though it is to be seen only in the occasional individual quarrel.

I remember two street scenes in Shanghai, from opposite ends of the spectrum of size, importance and grandeur. At the small end lies a suppertime scene in the crowded street near our apartment building on the grounds of Tong Ji Da Xue (Fellowship University). On one side of this Shanghai suburban street are several shops including a hardware-dry goods store capable of providing a TV set, cast iron woks and underwear, a barber shop and a food, cake and candy store. Across the twenty-foot-wide street, which teems with heavy

13

traffic from the docks to main roads, are a series of the hovel cottages of the type the city is gradually tearing down to replace with apartment buildings. A bicycle repair station and power air pump (2 cents to fill your tires) stand next to a two-room house in which a loud-mouthed and powerful looking middle-aged man with an iron-gray thatched brushcut, clad in khaki shorts and white undershirt, is having a fierce row with his harridan of a wife. Neither seems to give an inch in the flurry of waving arms and screamed anger but the ground belongs to the wife and the husband, still shouting in the open door and windows, retreats to sit on a stool outside, to be met by laughter and smiles from neighbors and passersby. The shouting dies down to occasional vicious exchanges and even as it continues a hand reaches out through the window and proffers a bowl of rice and chopsticks. The whole domestic explosion peters out to a muted ending as full mouths hamper the verbal joust.

On the other end of the Shanghai street scene lie the marvels of the thirty-fifth anniversary of the victory of the Communist Revolution on October 1, 1985. All of the foreigners had already been feted at a civic reception which featured some of the most exceptional buffet delicacies I have ever eaten. A monstrous Yellow Fish, presented upright rather than lying on his side and with working flashlight bulbs for eyes vies in my memory with wonderful dragons carved from melons. On the night of the anniversary we were taken through the humid streets (it had been 31 C. during the day) to view the first large fireworks displays in Shanghai since the Cultural Revolution. Traveling there in the ubiquitous Toyota van was the epitome of Shanghai streets at night. Literally millions of people were on the streets to celebrate and the van often slowed to a crawl as it passed through narrow roads. Houses, illuminated with their 60-watt bulbs and TV screens, presented a series of flashes of Shanghai domestic life as the van moved by. In one are four old people watching television, in others late cooking or children playing with young fathers or people finishing dressing, while outside other people are relaxing on the chaise lounges where they will sleep after the festivities.

The Exhibition Hall, which we reached after a stop for Cokes, tonic water and beer in the air-conditioned lounge of the Jin Jiang Hotel, is a five-story Stalin gothic building of an immense and strangely impressive ugliness. Atop it is a restaurant where many marriage feasts were in progress as many Chinese marriages take place on the few national holidays, October 1st and Spring Festival being favored. Outside, on a larger paved terrace with chairs and tables, the foreigners and their hosts assembled in a cooling breeze to drink beer or the ever-present jusiesway, orange soda pop, the same option as the Chinese really offer as their answer to the perennial Western question of what to drink with Chinese cooking. (Tea is rarely, if ever, offered with or immediately after meals in Shanghai.) The fireworks began against the skyline backdrop of buildings which had been outlined with lights for the anniversary. We were almost overlooking the People's Park, built on the site of the old racecourse just as the Exhibition Hall itself stands where Silas Hardoon, one of the Baghdad Jewish merchant princes (along with the Sassoons) once had his twenty-six acre garden park and residence.

The fireworks from the People's Park are surprising not only for their extraordinary floods of richly colored beauty and the fact that the display runs nearly two hours but chiefly for their silent glory against the velvet oriental night. It could have been that we were too far from the park but it seems more likely that Chinese fireworks are silent, painting sweeping strokes of abstract color for the eye alone. And the eyes surely feasted for there were no less than seven displays in various sectors of the vast city and all were in view from our sixth-story terrace if one walked around the perimeter of the restaurant.

What made the event strange and somewhat surreal against the semi-tropical night was that after about forty-five min-

15

utes the amazing display became mere background to a dance party and chatfest. Everyone talked and drank beer or the ubiquitous orange fizzy, but our Chinese hosts and the guests looking out of the restaurant where they were gorging on wedding banquets were obviously there to watch the foreigners cavort. Some of the Westerners, their inhibitions fully released by the festival atmosphere obliged, but I did not. The Chinese sometimes give the impression that they see foreigners as fish in bowls to be mused at and amused by, and nowhere is this more obvious than in the matter of dancing. Students and adults want their Westerners to dance (and sing, if possible) and they are shocked if adults do not want to do the twist or the two-step. From the Westerners' viewpoint two things are clear; that there is a *deja vu* aspect to the music and dancing (nothing is less than four or five years out of date and is performed with a wooden quality of imitation by Chinese dancers) and there is no comprehension of the sensual-erotic content of most Western popular music and dance. In fact all heavy rock and rough trade music was simply disliked by students and Susan ran up against very considerable teenage prudery when she used Prince's lyrics as an English comprehension exercise.

After the fireworks and the parapet balcony dance party it was suddenly back into the streets and home. I say suddenly because Chinese social events end on cue when everyone packs up and goes home. This is particularly true if there is transport laid on, of course (although, in keeping with socialist principles of equality there is a pleasant custom that the professional drivers always get to attend the events to which they transport us), but the Chinese completely avoid the silly verbal ballet of saying "Oh! Don't go yet." by simply rising and saying "I will go now." or "We must go now" and then promptly doing it.

So the night streets flow past the van, presenting once again the fascinations of a city which lives in its streets, where life flows continually, day and night, charged with the energy of the people of this busiest of all cities.

16

The Bicycle, The Bus and The Car

Shanghai is a city on the move. Its 12,000,000 residents plus an estimated 1,000,000 daily visitors, many of them peasants from the surrounding countryside coming into the city for the first time, seem to a Westerner all to be on the move at the same instant. There are simply no adequate adjectives to describe the human torrent pouring through the streets in daylight hours, but the citizens' myriad ways of getting from here to there are one of the great feasts for the eyes as well as presenting challenges of agility and endurance for the outsider.

Begin with the lowly bicycle. In Shanghai it is not lowly at all, but the object of as complicated a lore as the whole of the automobile syndrome in America. There are bicycles and there are bicycles, the best produced by two proud companies in Shanghai itself. I go to buy one at the Number Ten Department Store, shunning the simpler possibility of buying it in the Friendship Store where foreign tourists and foreign residents have the relative ease of not fighting the Chinese shopping crowds. I have investigated and discovered that even among these proud Shanghai companies, the makers of Golden Phoenix and Forever bicycles, there are fine lines of distinction as to the quality of the different models. The best and most coveted bicycle in Shanghai is the Golden Phoenix #14, whose gleaming black paint and writhing Phoenix symbol are better applied over the most solid and carefully built of the line. This Cadillac of bicycles is nearly $15 more expensive, at about $85 US, than its nearest rivals, the Golden Phoenix #18 or the Forever #13. Below these come a bewildering variety of model numbers and types, some featuring brightly colored paints or even three gears. I am warned against the three-speed model. It does not have good paint and, after all, Shanghai has almost no hills. The citizen of Shanghai wants durability above all in a bicycle. It is a once in a rare while purchase and all of the coveted brands require waiting until one's work unit provides a certificate allocating a purchase. You could buy an inferior import from another city but almost everyone waits for his turn to buy the local best.

At the Number Ten Department Store I find my Golden Phoenix #14, the king of bicycles. Like all Shanghai bicycles it is an almost perfect replica of a 1938 British Raleigh bicycle with a thick, very strong tube frame, and the characteristic full chain guard completely enclosing the chain. Its standard equipment includes a loud bell, which will join the continual chorus at every intersection as soon as I begin to ride, a kick stand, and, perhaps most importantly for the Shanghai user, a rear carrier strong enough to carry an adult or other notable loads. For a Shanghai bicycle is a beast of multiple burden and it is not at all unusual to see a father pedalling with his child in a seat attached to the center bar while his wife rides sidesaddle on the rear carrier with a handbag or small suitcase in hand.

But I am not to have these wonders, at least not in the form of a Golden Phoenix #14. The clerk explains, in the usual scraps of his English, my hopeless Chinese and a good deal of hand gesturing, that my bicycle certificate, while it is the powerful one issued to foreign experts (who are each entitled to one bicycle without having to wait for their certificate), is not powerful enough for a #14. I am offered everything else in the store. I decline.

When I return with a Chinese friend we end up in the manager's outer office, a vast conference room where we must sit down while an assistant discusses our problem on the phone with the bicycle factory. I still lose. After over an hour

18

of discussions I buy the consolation prize, a Golden Phoenix #18, accepting the most reasonable argument that they only issue enough #14 certificates each month to match the production, although one must still wander all over Shanghai to find a #14 to purchase.

Outside the #10 Department Store, in the center of Shanghai's busiest shopping area, I mount my Golden Phoenix. I ride, surrounded on every side by thousands of other bicycles, through throngs of pedestrians and beside the trucks and cars which fill every street. The noise, the shouting, the horns, the handcarts, men running with shoulder poles carrying baskets: the riding environment requires all the attention of a new rider. We have already seen too many accidents involving bicycles for me to assume that anyone, foreigner or not, has a particularly good chance of surviving on Shanghai's streets.

With the help of an American friend I go the next Saturday back to the city center to get a license. The bureau is open only Saturday *afternoon*, after the xiu xi (pronounced shu she—a restful mouthful of s's) or lunch rest which runs from 1130-1300 hrs. without fail in Shanghai. After waiting in fairly long lines (a half hour wait is very good for anything in Shanghai) twice the bicycle is branded by a marvelous punch press machine which stamps a serial number on the top center of the handlebars while I hold the bike's bum in the air, for the press requires the handlebars to be in the air. I then get a second branding done to the frame near the pedals by an old man wielding a hammer and individual letters which he stamps into the frame. I am then issued my license book, which like a British automobile license book of old will record all of the owners of the machine. In its neat, credit card-sized orange plastic case, adorned with a stylized drawing of a bicycle, I must have this license available to show the police at any time. I am also given a forty-page book of the rules of the road for cyclists. Needless to say I cannot read a single character of it. I doubt the Chinese read it either, a judgment based on my asking about to find out why I have been cautioned several times while riding my daughter Emma in her $2 wicker childseat mounted on the front frame bar behind the handlebars. Some opine that at four and one-half years of age she is too large. Some opine that there are certain main streets where bicycles must have only their principal riders. Some assert that you must get off and walk the bicycle when crossing an intersection or crossing a bridge in close proximity to traffic while carrying a child. Others do not know. Some suggest that it is dangerous. I wonder what the mysterious rules of the road book says. After two such warnings, of which I cannot understand a word, I stop taking Emma on roads where traffic policemen are to be encountered. Foreigners only get warnings, because the Chinese policemen want to be friendly and don't want the confusions of issuing tickets or confiscating bicycles. The only foreigners who get worse treatment lose bicycles they have parked illegally and have to locate them in a police compound. An "I don't understand" attitude usually gets the bicycle back without a fine.

Bicycle footpower serves Shanghai the way horsepower serves the West. A simple two-wheel bicycle with carrier and some cord permits the carrying of six fifteen-foot-long bamboo poles, wicker baskets filled with vegetables, geese, chickens, small manufactured products such as toys or gear wheels, briefcases, sacks, and a vast string of other bundles. In my Shanghai dreams I imagine one bicycle carrying all of these at once, the pedaler completely hidden but known to be present because the mountainous load slowly advances. A more advanced form involves two immense wicker panniers which hang almost to the ground beside the back wheels and which can be laden with pecks of market vegetables or vast quantities of fish or shrimp. In a city liberally dotted with small street markets the subdivision of products to be sold often comes down to these bicycle-sized loads.

The real beast of burden, however, is the three-wheeler. A

low flat cart with an iron railing is welded to the front end from a bicycle and driven by an elongated chain to the rear wheels. These are everywhere, laden so that you cannot see the driver except from the front. The loads can be two fifty gallon drums, walls of boxes which can reach as much as four feet above the driver's head and as much as ten feet in length if a few bamboo supports are added. The most spectacular loads are empty containers, particularly the red and white round cardboard cake boxes, loads one is certain are going to lift the drivers and flip them over backward. Less spectacular, but very heavy, are the large hot-water urns, carried in twos to every location where tea leaves await infusion in a city of tea drinkers.

The three-wheelers are also beasts of live burdens. The aged, adults and children ride them as ambulances or simply as common transport, often with an umbrella to keep off the fierce sun. One often sees a new sofa carried longways in one, husband pedalling furiously while proud wife and children sit in state on their new possession. Well, perhaps not pedalling furiously exactly, because with loads like that and no gearing the work is taxing and slow. I once saw a three-wheeler so heavily overloaded that it kept tipping backward, lifting the front wheel and the unfortunate driver into the air. Passersby would level it, the driver would progress, and it would tip again. But he had to carry on, for the load could not be left in the street.

The vast traffic of bicycles must contend for the streets with the flow of vehicles. To drive a motor vehicle in China you must be a professional, skilled in repairing the vehicle you drive and versed in the positively mystically complex rules of right-of-way in what initially appears to be a free-for-all with no rules at all. There are few if any private vehicles in the city and the drivers work for their danwei or unit which uses them as a motor pool. These drivers know, for example, that they must shut off their engines at all possible opportunities, and once up to speed, about 30 mph, they coast, pop-starting their vehicles by engaging the clutch as they begin to slow down. This measure is to reduce pollution in a city where it grays the sky and to save gasoline, for China, despite ample oil reserves, is conserving fuel very carefully and controlling its distribution. This stop, coast and start rule must tear the living daylights out of clutches and the electrical systems of vehicles. One morning the driver who came to take me to teach could not start and, with a knowledge born of bitter experience, lifted the hood and proceeded to pick bits of gear metal from the starter motor out of the engine compartment and from the ground beneath his two-year-old Shanghai Motorworks car. As another car took me to work I thought to myself that a part like that would probably be difficult to replace, given the pressure on supplies in China. The car was back on the road forty-eight hours later, suggesting that starter parts are inventoried at the unit's garage in the same way North American garages usually carry points and plugs.

The vast army of cyclists moving goods and the ease with which drivers make complex repairs are evidences of a key element of Shanghai's whole domestic economy. Labor, manpower, is the most available of all commodities. It is easier and wiser, given Shanghai's demands and population, to find men to repair a complex machine or men to pedal thousands of laden bicycles than it is to find more motor vehicles or to allocate more fuel to their endeavors. And while the Chinese speak of the need to modernize almost apologetically, as though nothing will get done until modernization, the foreigner in fact is marveling that this complex structure runs so well or that it runs at all. Shanghai is a fantastic industrial complex whose transport system is largely manpowered, and that fits in perfectly with the extremes of decentralization which places light to medium industry in every sidestreet and alley of the city, where it is serviced by the streams of three-wheelers as well as the trucks which wedge their ways everywhere.

The other ways that people move in Shanghai are by bus and by taxi, although the taxi transport is largely used by visitors. The bus system is taxed beyond the believable, with 11 people per square meter on the rush hour runs. Many of the busses are ancient, again kept in service by the devotion of the human element of drivers and repair personnel. Drivers, carefully watching temperature gauges, often stop to add water to radiators from large metal watering cans which they carry beside their seats. Most of the busses are articulated, and they even have two half-moon bench seats tucked into their accordion pleats. The crowds are so tight that at times you can relax completely standing up because there is simply nowhere to fall. As soon as the busses fill, the ticket takers are trapped at their stands fore and aft, so everyone helps pass money and tickets backward and forward to the customers. You call out what fare you want or flash a bus pass but it is primarily an honor system and occasional fierce arguments break out between the ticketakers, who are mainly vivacious young women, and someone who expects to travel free because he or she is crammed into a corner more or less out of sight. Then the Chinese attitude toward civil order and the conflicting desire for excitement come into play. Everybody enters the shouting argument and the polis, people in general, often force the situation to an honest resolution. Everyone shares in enforcing the rules either from this remarkable attitude of general responsibility or, in some cases, from the less admirable desire to not let anyone off when you are paying yourself. So the people, in the vast, crowded sense which that term has in Shanghai, take a role in the process of seeing fairness prevail.

The same thing can be seen operating in the dilemma of who sits down on the bus. Pregnant women get to sit down. The old usually get to sit. Anyone carrying a child gets to sit down with the child on lap. This does not always happen spontaneously, although it must be said that it frequently does. On other occasions the ticket collectors loudly demand and get seats for those who need them, using a mixture of command and scorn to clear a space. On occasion Emma or young Chinese children find themselves sitting on the ticket collector's small counters which are conveniently near the doors and to which the children can be passed when their parents have just squeezed in the doors and cannot even move through to get near a seat. In the matter of who sits down the foreigner runs into problems, because it proves to be almost impossible to give up a seat to an appropriate candidate. The action of trying to do so, however, often embarrasses someone else into getting up or draws the ticket takers' attention to the case.

Getting on the busses is a different matter. Here fierce pushing scrums occur because there are just so many people trying to use the system. Often the doors of the busses will not close because they are jammed with bodies, angry bodies determined to get aboard. In a city where so many people are so orderly so much of the time there seems to be an unwritten law that at the bus stop the rules of the game briefly change. It can be seen in peoples' eyes as the bus approaches. A moment is coming when the rules of co-existence will be briefly cancelled. Bodies tense and there are tiny jockeyings for position. The crush is on. This was not a great bother for me. At 6 feet, 1-1/2 inches I am a good deal bigger than most Chinese. But for the small and the aged it is a serious problem, one that the people of Shanghai worry about a good deal. At major bus loading points systems of lines with rails and marshalls are being used, but too many bus stops are on streets with narrow sidewalks where this is not possible.

The street traffic is kept moving partly by the old men's brigade. These gents form some sort of cadre, each of which is given a red armband and a whistle. They direct both traffic and pedestrians in many parts of the city and in busy areas there may be one on every streetcorner. They are neither the police who direct traffic and change streetlights from the elevated kiosks nor the police on motorcycles who attend to most ordinary disturbances or crimes. Although vested with authority of a sort they are clearly not vested with very much, and they are always getting into fierce arguments with people who won't obey them, particularly the cocky delivery boys who tear through the city on tattered bicycles.

On the Huai Hai Lu, a broad plane tree-lined street in the old French Concession which is the most sophisticated shopping street in the city, I witnessed a minidrama involving the old gent's brigade. I turned from a shop window when I heard fierce whistling and shouting on the street. Looking toward it I saw a series of the old gentlemen, stretching perhaps two blocks at one-hundred-yard intervals, all blowing whistles and shouting. The object of their attentions, a young man on a bicycle, was in front of me at that instant, pedalling furiously and making a sudden turn into a side street across the road. There he ran into grief, colliding with the press of pedestrians crossing the intersection. As the nearest of the old men ran towards him he sought to escape, but the crowd held him. The real police were then summoned and he was taken away in a van, plucked from the magical instant crowd of 250.

The incident is typical of several things in the city. The young man, who had either stolen the bicycle or was simply riding it on Huai Hai Lu, where the bus traffic and flood of pedestrians make riding illegal during the business day, was apprehended by the crowd, then by the paralegal old gentlemen and finally by the police. Once again the polis, the people themselves, acted as the law and held the criminal.

The action of everyone acting as the law seems to be one of the aspects of Shanghai, and probably China, which most clearly separates its civil order from that in North America. In talks with our Chinese friends and in a long discussion about Chinese law that I carried on with my students, a picture emerged of people who act when they see something illegal happening. There are block committees which settle residential disputes and domestic problems, and in cases of theft or violence there are almost always enough fellow citizens to help hold a suspect until official police help arrives. People see it as their duty to see law and order enforced and, of course, the police would be hopelessly outnumbered if this were not the case.

Shanghai is remarkable because its citizens are, in the main, so law abiding and so able to cooperate in the vast confusion of the metropolis. And many of the minor violations generate situations rather than thoughtless applications of law.

A young man on a bicycle has a partial collision with a pedestrian before me on a quiet street. The pedestrian and his friend hold the bicycle and a long shouting argument ensues. Passersby join in and then move on as the argument drags on for five, ten, fifteen minutes. The injured party, his pantleg is soiled, wants to take the cyclist to the police but he and his friend are strong enough to hold the youth and the bicycle but not strong enough to drag the resisting offender away. The impasse ends as a surly fuss in which the cyclist, momentarily freed after being held for nearly twenty minutes, escapes while still arguing with and cursing the two men as he drives away. In this case the people in the streets were clearly not convinced that it was worth the trouble, and their refusal to help amounted to a judgment of the case.

In fact, it seems as though a lot of the popular justice functions to keep people out of the hands of the formal legal apparatus, a shadow of the former fears of the law in China generated by centuries of oppressive and corrupt Imperial courts. It is still felt by my students that if a man is tried for a crime he is probably guilty of it although a form of Western adversary law is now coming into being in China. Most trials consist of confessions and a parade of character witnesses—workmates, neighbors, work leaders—before a sentence is passed. These confessions are not likely to be the archetypal confession under torture of the dictatorial communist regime (a concept which the reality of China with its vast, varied and really very free peoples makes into a joke or a piece of right wing wind) but simply an admission once overwhelming evidence has been presented to the accused before the trial. The confession clears the way for the court to assess the person, the gravity of the offense and the appropriate punishment.

Once in the hands of the courts the Chinese criminal is in real trouble. We saw or heard of perhaps a dozen barred bus loads of criminals, their heads shaved, a few probably going to execution but the majority being shipped to the North. The death penalty is very much alive in China and while it would be impossible to guess at its effect on the crime rate, it gets applied to factory managers and minor bureaucrats accused of economic crimes such as graft as well as to crimes of violence. There is a great deal of publicity showing the punishment of major crimes, with photographs of the criminals and news stories appearing on the local public notice boards along with the pages of the daily newspapers which the citizens frequently stop to read.

Many more Chinese criminals suffer a fate worse than death: imprisonment in a prison city on the frontier accompanied by permanent exile to that same city once the sentence is complete. With the vital and intensive Chinese family life and, in the case of Shanghai, a New York-like sense that everywhere else is unbearably backward and provincial, exile from the place of one's birth must be the most effective deterrent the authorities could ever devise. As with the attitude toward settling disputes outside the formal law, this practice of exile has a long history in Chinese law, being the fate of nobility who fell from fortune in the ancient empires. The nobles were, however, able to put a better face on it, for they retreated to Buddhist contemplation and the writing of poetry on their country estates. But today the threat of a life-long exile in a country where travel restrictions can enforce it must deter many from crime. Minor offenders serve terms in local prisons where several of my fellow teachers, on a prisons' tour I missed, saw the amusing and enlightening sight of lightly-guarded prisoners making locks and doing woodcarving with mean-looking axes.

Crime and transportation come together in Shanghai in the amazing circumstance of the bus that stops in the police station. Yes, *in* the police station. Shanghai is a city with very talented pickpockets and their opportunities are particularly rewarding and worth the risk of having the real violence of the law down upon them. For the Chinese carry plenty of cash money with them in order to take instant advantage of any opportunity to buy consumer goods that are often in short supply but come to shops in sudden truckload lots. We were constantly amazed by the sums of money in Chinese wallets considering the annual incomes. The problem is aggravated by the fact that many peasants come into the city carrying big bankrolls (obtained as a result of the new free market rates for farm produce) to shop for some special item. In any event Shanghai pickpockets, who we were told train their quick and delicate touch by learning to move live hot coals with grace and rapidity, work the busses where the crowding makes it very difficult to tell if one is being burgled. But if you do realize you have lost your bankroll you cry out, or at least the Chinese do, and then the bus goes straight, non-stop to the courtyard of the main police station where it is emptied very carefully under the steely gaze of the law. If the thief has not departed the bus before the theft was discovered the money is usually found on the floor of the bus at the police station, covertly dropped by the thief so it will not be found on his person in the body search which ensues for the passengers if the money is not on the floor of the bus. Two of my colleagues had their wallets or purses stolen in the city (although they were not sure if it was on the busses) but foreigners usually get passports and wallets back, sans the money, because pickpockets drop them in postboxes rather than be found with them. Stealing from foreigners is likely to be a capital offense. So while the bicycle may be a risky form of personal transport in the dazzling confusion of Shanghai's

28

streets (the Flying Pigeon bicycles were jokingly renamed the Sitting Ducks by foreigners), it is at least a safe assumption that even the hot coal-trained Shanghai pickpocket will not reach you as you wheel through the exciting streets.

What Did We Do?

What did we do with our days in Shanghai? Well, Susan and I worked in the mornings, and on some of the afternoons. But the features of at least two days a week were the expeditions downtown. On those days we would take the Tongji minibus at 1345 hrs, crammed in merrily with our German and American and Swiss fellow apartment dwellers. The bus went first to the Foreign Food Store which would go from empty to full with the arrival of twelve or fifteen of us with bags and baskets. Then would follow an orgy of tomato examination and potato squeezing and the usual ritual of asking whether there was any cheese yet. Frozen fish would appear, whole, as would frozen chickens who had paused long enough to lose their feathers and innards but not their accusing heads. Confused conversations in broken English and wretched Chinese would be rescued by amateur interpreters, while other parties would oogle strange herbs done up in paper (in fact the Shanghaiese use little besides salt, pepper, ginger, five spice powder, and monosodium glutemate). Wise counsellors would advise that garlic is sold as shoots rather than cloves in Shanghai, or that baking powder has a special Chinese name or that those green fruits were oranges, not treated to make them orange of skin. On one occasion the word was passed that unheard of delicacies—cream cheese, gouda, and cheddar cheese—had come to Shanghai on a cruise ship and were being sold to friends through friends. The supplies were snapped up instantly.

Then it was back on the bus with bags stowed under the seats. Some only put their groceries on and stayed in that

30

part of the downtown for other errands but most rode on up to the Jin Jiang Hotel in the old French Concession to shop on Huai Hai Lu or at the hotel shops, particularly at Jessica's, a Japanese-run importer of foods, toys, drugs, and Western and Japanese foods. While we shopped there or simply drank ice cold beer in the hotel lounge and watched the tourists—such strange creatures in inappropriate bright plumage—the bus made a trip to the dairy for the Tongji milk supply. Then at 1700 we boarded the bus and returned to the downtown to pick up some of the others at the Friendship Store, another shopping place for foreigners, and it was back through the rush hour traffic to home, where those who had not stayed with the bus appeared like magic to claim the groceries they had left aboard. On one occasion I forgot this vital pickup and our groceries rotted for three days in the bus terminal, causing some nasty rows between wai bans as we urged action and leading ultimately to the return of the whole decayed mass for us to throw away all but the canned goods and spend two days scrubbing out the cordura bag which had held part of the load. On this occasion the wai ban never did solve the problem but Si Ayi, incensed at the waste, shouted down the officials at the depot and recovered the groceries.

The favorite variation on the downtown outing was to visit the Jin Jiang Club, a private club from the French occupation days now open to foreigners only. In its vast, wood paneled interior lurked a wonderful swimming pool which conjured the past glories of Shanghai. A hand-tiled monster, larger than Olympic size and never crowded, its deserted galleries conjured memories of coffee and cakes and cocktails and musicians who must have played on the bandstand at one end. With its high translucent glass hangar-shaped roof it provided an island, or rather a lagoon of calm and relaxation. There was also an eight-lane bowling alley with up-to-date Brunswick equipment and a convenient bar which allowed a plunge out of Shanghai for an hour or two. Upstairs was an amazing ballroom where the foreign teachers and their hosts had an afternoon Christmas dancing party. It has or had, because the Jin Jiang Club was purchased by Japanese interests and was closed for extensive and unknown renovations in the Spring of 1985, a sprung dancefloor which made dancing an experience much like floating and was another throwback to the luxuries enjoyed by the occupiers in the days before the Revolution.

There were other attractions that warranted outings in the city, such as the Art Gallery and the Old Chinese city, but for us the chief attraction was shopping. In the summer our party consisted of Emma in her stroller with the rest of us riding shotgun through the crowded streets. If we saw something we wanted we would turn into a shop and then the fun would begin. Everyone, and everyone always meant mobs, wanted to see what we were buying, and people would actually crowd between us and the counters to get a look. They also wanted to touch Emma, particularly her blond hair, so we worked out a phalanx system with Emma in the middle with her face nearly touching the display case glass and us surrounding her on three sides. Then the overworked clerks would be the only ones who could reach her, and their fascination assured us of rapid service. Candy stores, toy stores, children's clothing stores, and bakeries yielded to this approach, and we soon learned to try on everything possible on the spot, as it is hard to do exchanges when you don't speak the language.

When I was shopping alone matters were easier and my two favorite purchases were a *son et lumiere* combination. In one vast electrical goods store, which sold everything from fuses to generators, I bought two bankers' lamps, the brass ones with the green glass shades. The purchase nearly fell through because it was 1730 hrs. and I had to go to a central cashier to pay the $30 U.S. (68Y) for the pair. The cashiers had decided to shut so a crowd and I found ourselves waving slips and money at them in their glass enclosure while they calmly picked up purses and coats. They relented, however, when they saw the foreigner, and I got out with my two lamps in their styrofoam boxes belted together with one of the lightning acts of string tying that is a feature of Chinese shopping. I value those lamps enormously because I then had to carry them to a dinner party at the Peace Hotel and on a pub crawl which ended at the Seaman's Club, a wild and wooly joint which concentrates the waterfront action in a city which is thin on nightlife. When I finally reeled in our apartment door after the fastest bus ride I have ever taken (made hilarious by our drunken condition and attempts to take pictures which ended up as shots of the roof and floor) I was certain that I had a collection of green glass shards with me. But no, they survived that trip and the longer one in a shipping crate to Canada.

The other half of my *son et lumiere* pair was a large brass gong from the music store on Nanjing Lu. I lusted after this for months, as I lusted after all of the Chinese string instruments in the window which were on sale for absurdly low prices. Susan talked me out of the strings by pointing out that I am entirely unmusical, but I can beat a brass gong with the best of them and it now echoes through the halls of our home occasionally but with great effect.

What we did when we were not downtown was less venturesome but sometimes fascinating. The polyglot mix of children flowed constantly around our building and the large bag of Lego we had brought with us was virtually worn out in a year. We cooked a good deal, and I rediscovered the joys of preparing vegetables with geometries. As chief peeler I worked on potatoes of the strangest shapes, soothing myself after hard days by making nice, regular chips out of bent and skewed shapes. I cut up some of the smallest green peppers I ever hope to see. Unlike Beijing Shanghai does not live on cabbage through the winter but it is often reduced to root vegetables which require a good deal of washing off and trimming. I also rediscovered, with not quite as much enthusiasm, the joys of washing dishes, although Mike became a very unwilling assistant and took over half of the job. Liquid dish soap is one product that is most readily available in Shanghai.

As a baby sitter I must have read Emma five hundred stories, including plenty of the English versions of Chinese children's stories that are readily available with lovely illustrations. Mike ploughed through the whole of *The Journey to the West*, the great saga of the Monkey King and his amazing adventures. Monkey is at the center of Chinese childhoods, appearing in cartoons, as a figure at every childrens' party and in the amazing puppet plays which are now being revived with their ancient and elegant special effects. His great antiquity shames Mickey Mouse, although Disney cartoons are popular on Chinese television.

Emma and Mike also pitched in, taking in turn the task of going across to the canteen at the other building to get eggs, milk, bread and quarts of beer. The canteen was closer than any corner store, but it was altogether a riskier venture. The eggs, which did not travel in nice safe cardboard cartons, had to be individually examined for cracks and later individually broken into a dish before being added to other ingredients to avert the minor disaster of a single rotten egg in the bunch. But Emma, at 4, never spilled a basket of eggs and was a great favorite with the kitchen staff. Mike, who at 11 was a typical boy who had got into such things as the coal pile and onto such illegal places as the roof, had a rougher relationship with the canteen staff, but his Chinese was surer and the results of his errands more certain. Emma became a heavy bug collector in Shanghai and I became skilled at popping holes in jar lids with my penknife and at disposing of the wispy dead and their dried-out leafy environments. Shanghai brought out all of the primitive children's entertainments, in which Mike tended to lead exploits and Emma, the smallest of the children old enough to be on her own, could always be found quite happily running furiously just behind everybody else. I sometimes felt vaguely guilty at taking children to China, particularly when the cries of boredom were heard in the dead of winter, but as I now hear the same cries in the midst of the plenty of home I do not think the year did any harm. In any event, Disneyland California lay as a golden promise over our last months in Shanghai, a promise that was paid in full, with bonus candy, on return.

One of our chief adult home entertainments was talk, a tiny fragment of the enormous rumor mill which grinds among foreigners in Shanghai, as well as the opportunity to get teaching advice and present, on occasion, coffee sent from Canada (I liked Chinese coffee just fine but I was not in a majority) or delicacies found in bakery shops. We formed a one-table bridge night, although the bridge sometimes degenerated into talking and drinking. The quiet of the late evenings, except for the frogs' chorus in spring and the occasional bid, was a pleasant antidote to the action and noise of the Shanghai day. In winter it was even more pleasant because our flat was cozy (partly because I sealed the leaky windows around with fibreglass tape) and every one of us had spent a bracing day teaching in unheated buildings.

Amidst all of the activity I developed one routine which I look back on most fondly. In the long autumn evenings I would take one of the excellent Chinese cigars and wander down to the stone table with stone seats under the plane tree outside our building. And there I would do something I do not get to do anywhere else: I would smoke and do absolutely nothing. Time did not stand still in Shanghai, it was not Shangri-la. But there was a time, once work was done, to do nothing. After all, I had no lawn to mow, no fuses to fix, no committees to prepare for. I could do nothing about my consumer debt (and besides, my creditors were on the other side of the world) nor could I "advance my career." I could just sit and soak up the long Shanghai twilight. And I did.

Foray Posture

I have now eaten turtle soup, about which nothing whatsoever was mock. There he was, shell, claws, head and all, floating tummy up in a large steaming bowl in front of myself, Susan and my colleagues in a restaurant set in a tea plantation outside of Hangzhou, an ancient beauty spot some three and a half hours from Shanghai. And while his broth was quite delicious I'm afraid his very "wholeness" may have put me off eating him, for I found him a bit tough, very hard to manage and not, finally, a delicacy. But then I find lobsters in the shell equally not worth the work, so my bias may simply be toward quick foods like eels and squids and chickens whose eyes do not seem menacingly fixed upon me from the pot.

This chapter is not about food, primarily, but about the side trips out of Shanghai which were part of our time spent there, and which formed the punctuation marks in the months we spent in the city. It will not be a catalogue of individual trips but a blended description of the excitements, frustrations and curiosities of making forays into the cities and the countryside near Shanghai. I have called it Foray Posture because, like warriors at the ready on a probing expedition, we found sense and safety in expecting all that we could and being as ready as possible if our ventures were to prove a success.

Trips from Shanghai began at the Peace Hotel, a week or so before departure, with the ordering of soft seat train tickets. Soft seat is just what it sounds like, a section with reserved soft seats as opposed to hard seats, the wooden benches which are crammed full in the style of the pictures one often sees in newsreels of the Orient. Soft and hard seats are, of course, the way of saying first and second class in a country without classes. The tickets ordered at the hotel are available two or three days later, for someone actually goes and gets them physically at the main railway station and brings them back to the hotel. The first time you get them you discover the hardest fact about travel by rail in China: there are no return tickets. This means that every weekend spent outside of Shanghai begins, on arrival, with a trip to the foreigners' ticket office (as opposed to the public ticket lines in which people may wait hours) to arrange the trip back before the seats are all sold. Trains run often on the main lines, but they run full.

On one occasion Bob, one of our teaching colleagues who had come to Hangzhou on the same weekend we did, was simply unable to get a ticket to go back to Shanghai. We had got tickets because our wai ban had so messed up planning for the trip that higher officials at the Institute had stepped in and arranged for a government official to help us in Hangzhou. We offered Bob Emma's ticket, planning to put her on a lap or pay for a spare seat, and in that configuration the five of us boarded a crowded Sunday night express which stopped at Hangzhou. We found someone else in our seats and in the ensuing argument the lady conductors tried to put all of us off the train because, as it turned out, the official who had "helped" us had bought tickets for the wrong night (Saturday rather than Sunday) and we had no reservations at all. As some friendly Americans had been in "our" seats and had wonderfully "fitted" themselves elsewhere in the coach so our tired children and I could sit down and dump our mound of luggage, we prepared to operate on possession being nine tenths of the law while Susan argued with the conductors. They in turned called in armed railway police to throw us off the train but after the police saw the steam issuing out of Susan's ears they decided that it would not do to shoot a rabid mad dog foreign lady in a major railway station in front of Japanese and some American tourists and the train pulled away with all of us aboard. We finally placated the conductor ladies by showing great willingness to pay the extra fare and by letting them get to know Emma, who mustered a slightly tired version of her sweet little blond foreign child routine.

To return to preparations for a foray from Shanghai. Once the tickets are in hand you pack, and either buy or borrow a guidebook to where you are going. If you get a driver or a guide in China you may be sadly surprised at how little he or she will know, particularly if you go beyond the prepared spiel. This is a saddening phenomenon, one of those things which remind one of the sharpness with which the Chinese have turned on their history and cultural artifacts in the last few generations, although this is now changing. Food is also packed for the trip, for the trains provide hot water or tea but most riders grab food from vendors at the stops or carry bundles or boxes with them. We usually packed fruit, crackers, peanut butter, cheese (if available), ham (in cool weather), hard boiled eggs, butter, coffee sachets, chocolate and soft drinks, the smaller items in the handy aluminum boxes which the Chinese use for a two li measure of rice. On one occasion we watched a Japanese tour party around us in a train systematically and tidily demolishing very substantial and identical box lunches at a moment when we had underplanned and were sustaining ourselves on tea and soft drinks till we should arrive back in Shanghai on Sunday evening.

Once prepared, the next task was to get to the train on time. This required booking a taxi the day before at the Peace Hotel, because telephone booking was risky and the taxis foreigners can get are dispatched from the tourist hotels. Usually the taxi was late, and there was very little one could do but wait and hope. Once at the station it was into the foreigners' entrance and lounge and then onto the train with ease. Well, it should have been ease but it is then discovered that the seats on the train are not numbered in the same sequence as the tickets, so there is often a good deal of jockeying about in order that foursomes may sit together. A good spirit usually prevailed in these matters except when the rearrangement might involve a party of tourists, who sometimes were nervous and uncertain enough to be unwilling to switch. Some of the American tourists in China come there to satisfy themselves that a socialist country must be a horrible dictatorship with a Commie with a Tommy Gun just waiting for you to switch seats in a railway car.

I could probably offer a vast number of those stories of minor irritation which are a part of any traveler's life in a country where he doesn't speak the language and people's expectations of the normal differ radically from his; but I would prefer to remember some of the magic moments and try to offer them to you.

Our arrival in Suzhou (with Susan's sister and niece who had come half way around the world to visit us) was less than happy. Suzhou (Soochow in the old Anglicization) is an ancient city less than two hours from Shanghai. After the usual wait to buy tickets back to Shanghai we discovered fierce competition between different cab drivers to take us to the hotel, which was nice, but we then discovered that there were no taxis behind the offer, only pedicabs with wiry but tough youths to do the pedaling. A price was struck (by this time Susan's Chinese was equal to the rough and tumble) and two pedicabs, each with one child and two adults, set off for the hotel, which turned out to be nearly three miles from the station. The pedicab is a strange vehicle, a sort of rolling political allegory for the state of China today. The driver is not so demeaned as to have to run in the shafts like a rickshaw driver (we never saw a true rickshaw in China) but he still is essentially a beast of transport in a society where machines are relatively scarce (in Shanghai motorized bicycles are being converted to pedicabs). These young pedalers were archetypal pushy entrepreneurs and by the time we got to the hotel compound we had agreed to hire them for the afternoon to take us around for a fee which fluctuated through wild bursts of bargaining, one cab overtaking the other so the drivers could consult with each other while the passengers consulted with each other, and was finally nailed in place partly through the frequent handing out of Western cigarettes, some of which these thin, tough sweating human motors managed to smoke while running through the streets and shouting abuse and warning at everyone before them. Their courage melted at the hotel, however, for they were not supposed to be transporting foreigners at all and they left us at the gateway where we promised to meet them after lunch.

They took us to the pagoda, which was large, imposing, and rather boring until Emma, then only four, ran off up the stairs after her brother. I had gone up alone first and already come down the dangerous stairs. The top of this building was at least ten regular stories and I went up the second time at very high speed, a good test for a chronic asthmatic. Emma was only about three stories up but I took a pretty firm grasp on her hand for the walk down.

Suzhou's fame rests on its classical gardens, of which over one hundred remain. Our pedicabs took us to several but they were, in a sad way, disappointing. These beautiful places, carefully preserved and maintained, were originally the preserves of single families, who, in spaces of several acres or so, created endlessly varied and wonderfully amusing gardens full of revealed vistas come on suddenly around corners or glimpsed through the imaginatively shaped windows. Rock formations, some large enough to walk through or over, were interlaced with dwarf trees and strategically placed flowers to tease the mind and enchant. They must have been, when each was the preserve of a single family, places of silent contemplation and quiet conversation between lovers or scholars. What sadly ruins them today is that they are now public, an admirable political fact but wholly destructive to their atmosphere as they are always thronged by literally thousands of Chinese tourists with their penchant for snackfoods and the photographing of one another in strange and often dangerous locations. The resulting assault ruins the calm, a conundrum of freedom and equality versus elegance and the brutality of an oppressive history.

Why then is this one of my magic memories of touring in China? It is because we chanced, on the day after our pedicab odyssey, on the Garden of the Master of Fishing Nets at the noon hour when no Chinese is doing anything but eating or napping. It was only a long block from our hotel and its extraordinary delicacy and beauty are forever in my mind, as is its silence. Built originally in 1140 A.D., it was restored in 1770 and it is a *living* proof of the wisdom of ancient China. The two most modern things within its precincts only added to its beauty. One was a display of classical painting and calligraphy managed by a lady professor from the nearby University, who added her own grace to the garden, and the other was a display of contemporary Chinese lithographs of such stunning beauty, delicacy and technique that we made a return trip to Suzhou almost solely to return to the beauties of the garden and purchase two prints to carry across the world to our living room. The divinity of that quiet and elegant acre of garden which seemed to go on for a pleasant eternity through turns and windows and views, was for me the elegant little door in the wall of modern China which suggested the quality of the culture upon which China so proudly rests.

Ironically, our second visit to the Garden of the Master of Fishing Nets was in a different key that mixed the classical and the modern. I was stunned at a first view around a corner of a fully dressed Sung Dynasty maiden and could hardly catch my breath to decide whether I had been transported through time before, following her, I beheld the latest in television camera equipment filming a scene for a historical drama. The second trip through the garden was not so tran-

41

quil, but the shock of seeing its "living ghosts" forms a part of that most pleasant of memories.

Our most ambitious outing was to Wuxi and Yixing. Wuxi mixes the old and the new China and was most remarkable for us because we could not get reservations at the Tai Lake Hotel or any of the other Western Hotels and instead ended up in an immense room, nay, suite of rooms, at the Liangxi Hotel, which is usually used by overseas Chinese visiting China. It featured some of the best cooking we ate while traveling and was clearly one of the mausoleum-like structures erected during the 1950's when the Russians were influencing Chinese building. From there we sought out the CITS tourist service office to arrange a car and permit to travel to Yixing. The office was nearly invisible, an unmarked door in a stone wall behind the bus depot which we walked past several times before venturing into a charming tiny garden and an elegant old house. In China, you must be curious and persistent to tour successfully. Once inside we were shown great, if slow, courtesy, and discovered that we could go with car and driver to the Yixing Guesthouse and be met there by the required guide. The permit was never mentioned and we presume to this day that it really amounts to notifying CITS that you are traveling to an area where foreigners do not usually go.

We went to Yixing to see its pottery works, for it has great fame for its beautiful terra cotta teapots and other wares. Before we saw them, however, our young guide insisted that we tour some local scenic caves and eat lunch. The factory tour came only after a visit to a pottery museum but it was worth waiting for. In large, quiet clean workshops the pots are assembled, not thrown. Strips of the clay are delicately bent into exquisite shapes and decorated with sculptured features such as bamboo leaves and dragons. The factory store was a let-down after seeing the variety of the manufacture, for so much of the output is commissioned for Japan and other places that the nicest items we had seen being made were not for sale. Nevertheless we did all right

42

shopping there, despite an argument over a stiff charge they tried to levy for a cardboard packing carton and having to fight off a regiment of Japanese tourists, who are without doubt the world's fiercest shoppers. The nicest touch of our visit was to a local pottery store where we really found much better variety, perhaps because they got stock from more of the thirty-five potteries in town. Moreover, as they did not usually sell to foreigners we were a pleasant surprise in their roomy, cool shop where we browsed, surprised them with the number of pots we wanted (we were busy mentally ticking off most of our souvenir list as we stood there), and had the assistance of the pleasant young girl who had acted as our interpreter on the trip. We almost filled the trunk of the Toyota sedan that we had come in, a fact I lived to regret when we had to manhandle the whole lot onto the train at Wuxi and off of it in Shanghai.

My magic moments on the Wuxi trip, however, were not in Yixing, much as I would recommend that expedition as a chance to see the countryside and the pottery. Rather, it was a kindness, a song, and a night forage which stay with me as the mental markers of that trip. The kindness occurred because we decided to go the four miles to the Lake Tai Hotel for dinner in the evening and no taxi could be got out from town at 9:30 P.M. to take us back. After a three quarter of an hour wait in the hotel lobby, and with our children overtired and very difficult, the hotel staff arranged for us to go back in a car with one of the hotel's managers who was going off duty. It was a fairly desperate situation, as the hotel was full and we were well and truly stranded. It was very kind indeed for the tired hotel staff, who had no doubt contended all day with tourist demands, to make that one extra effort for us.

The next day we took the cruise on Lake Tai, which is the great, softly-lit beauty spot that we had been told it was. The cruise boat is very luxurious and there were stops to walk about several of the lovely islands. But it was on our return journey that a lovely young girl who was with a party of elderly and very distinguished looking officers of the People's Army, stood up and sang for them "Taihu Mei" (Beautiful Lake Tai) in a delicate and lovely voice. Not even the party of Japanese tourists who quickly descended upon her and forced her, by relentless urging, to sing again for their portable video cameras and microphones could ruin the original and wonderful spontaneous moment of her first rendition.

On our last night in Wuxi a minor crisis led to my final pleasant memory. The Liangxi Hotel had failed us at breakfast because it served only the Chinese fare of pickled beans, cold chicken, and bean paste dishes which neither we nor the children could cope with to start the day. So I walked out into the warm quiet dark evening (there are few streetlights in Wuxi) heading for the night market mentioned in the guidebook. It was closed, but nearby there was a store where I bought pastries and some fruitstands where I bought apples. In the night, in this town, the foreigner was not noticed, so my stroll was free from the glare of identity which haunted us everywhere and I could look on as people strolled about or chatted. And, I confess, I could look into the lighted, open-to-the street houses and see domestic moments in the calm tranquility of the evening. In China, I think, it is almost always moments of quiet that one remembers, moments when one is not formally looking as a tourist, but looking as a person at persons and the ordinary texture of their lives.

Our trips all ended with a burst of feverish action, for no matter how late we arrived in Shanghai there was always a mob scene at the station and a fierce struggle for a taxi. I often found myself in a crowd of about two hundred trying to get a taxi at a stand where a manager with a microphone instructed each driver who pulled up on who to take. Foreigners were always jumped in the line but the manager would load several Chinese customers, usually old people or tired mothers with babies before placing me ahead of the others. It was embarrassing to be thus treated and yet, tired as I always was at this point, I was always grateful. Efforts at phoning for the foreigners' taxis from the foreigners' lounge never succeeded at night. Then it was through the busy, dark streets of "home" to our quiet apartment and perhaps a cup of tea and an examination of tourist treasures.

I began this chapter speaking of turtle, and I should close with a fair judgment of the wonderful meal at the new restaurant in the tea plantation outside Hangzou of which he was a part. This was on a trip given us by our Institute, with our Chinese and foreign colleagues along. The meal was amazing and the setting calm and lovely, but it was there that I made a classic foreigner's mistake. On a walk we took before dinner I could not resist taking a handful of water from a clear running hill stream that bubbled through the plantation. I paid for it, spending the next day with a mild fever, a nasty headache and a stomach turned over by a giant hand mixing dough in my innards. As one of my American colleagues kindly remarked when I took the drink, the stream was probably someone's ox trough three miles further up the hillside. It was on that same trip that we were deep in the bowels of some wonderful Chinese caves when the lights went out, providing us and several hundred Chinese tourists with a very anxious five minutes in the dark bowels of the earth. But it was cool and wonderful in the caves, much more pleasant than later in the day when the minibus broke down and we spent half an hour in the hot countryside while the driver confirmed his rating as a mechanic and put things to rights. There is excitement to be had touring in China but the awkward moments always give way to kindnesses and discoveries and solutions, helped to a great extent by the Chinese will to be gracious to guests, however absurd their requests may be.

A modern apartment building with hangings

A twelve-story bamboo scaffold

A city center Shanghai residential street with hangings

The rice-popping machine

icycle Power — Susan with Emma in her seat on the Golden Phoenix #18

49

The author with his senior students in the Institute garden

50

A canal in Suzhou

Bicycle power (but not a three-wheeler)

The author with Emma at the botanical gardens

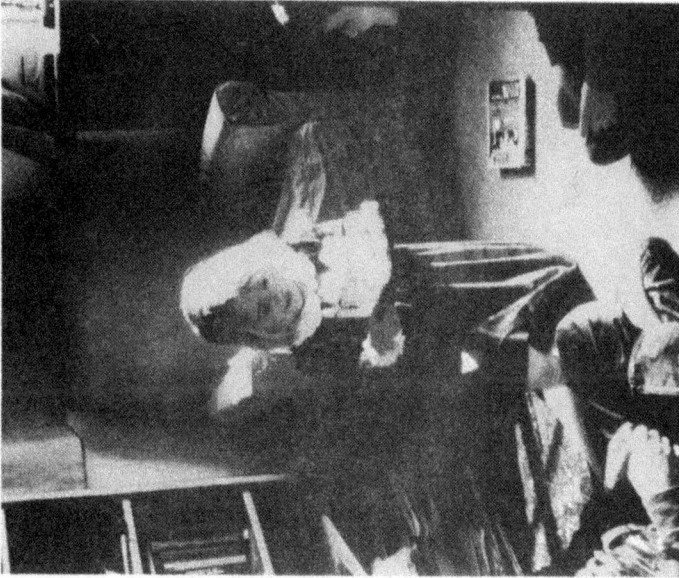

Emma's fourth birthday in our apartment

The Amusement Park — problems with English

PARAT ROOPER

Bride and groom with our children

Bicycle Power — two hot water urns on a three-wheeler

Getting Married

Chinese frogs come far closer to the Westerner's idea of the erotic than do the Chinese people. What sounded like a hundred thousand frogs lived in the two-acre market gardening patch of plots of land that were worked by our neighbors. At night in the spring and early summer they declared their desire in positively thunderous tones which would go on for hours, stopping for half an hour (while they sprayed their throats?) and bursting once again into a paean of desire. We each had our favorites. One was a basso profundo, obviously built like a middle linebacker. In contrast to his deep-throated violent desire were several urgent young comers with bursts of vocal desperation lasting for shorter intervals. Behind such stars was the chorus, all vastly interested in the production of little frogs in the joyful dark of the night. The honesty of their passions seemed so clear to us in comparison to the courting and marriage practices of our hosts which are the subject of this confused and bemused chapter.

Love and marriage in China have obviously been the subject of as much change in the past decades as any of the other institutions in the turmoil. But perhaps it is possible to perceive some elements which are constant and often admirable.

To begin: marriage in China is seen very much as a partnership and not as an occasion for the erotic. The number of Chinese couples who live apart for years at a time and remain celibate is astounding. Work assignments in different places, older students sent abroad without spouses and children (not, I think, a political hostage system but mainly due to the extraordinary problems in getting allocated enough foreign exchange to travel and study abroad), and the cataclysm of the Cultural Revolution have all tested the institution of marriage and found its truth in loyalty rather than in bed.

Among my students is one fine young man whose wife lives in a different province where he met and married her when he was sent down during the Cultural Revolution. Their five-year-old son lives with his grandparents in Shanghai. It is a cause for immense celebration when she wins a place in an engineering school in Shanghai and therefore receives permission from the authorities to move to the city where her husband and child live. She is an exception to a general policy formulated at the end of the Cultural Revolution to help prevent China's urban areas from overflowing, a policy which said that if someone from a city had married in the countryside neither they nor their spouse could ever return to that city to live. In another case a professor wins a place at Kansas University and she must leave her husband and two daughters for one or perhaps two years to lecture and study. This is a tremendously ambivalent event for it is a great honor and privilege to be chosen to go, but an enormous wrench to leave the comfort of the close-knit Chinese family. For most people in this position the care of children is not the primary concern because the extended family which is the Chinese way means that there will be grandparents and others to assist in actual care, but the wrench is nonetheless very great.

The longevity and loyalty of marriages are generally admirable but there are exceptions, of course. Divorce is powerfully discouraged, at the first level of defense by members of local block committees and by one's work unit. The scarlet creature of contemporary China is one who commits "third person interference"—the other woman (infrequently the other man) who steals a marriage partner. The authorities see this as a growing problem as it is particularly prevalent in the first few years of marriage. It is officially an immoral act and one which is punished by the courts and by all sorts of penalties in the work unit. While there is evidence that it is mainly the difficulties of young couples in adjusting to marriage which leads men or women to seek other partners, the official view, supported by frequent newspaper stories of men or women giving up a "third person" to return to their legal spouse, is that third persons are guilty parties wholly responsible for marriage collapse. Considering that divorcees and widows are still virtually unmarriageable in contemporary China makes an observer realize just how strong the desire to leave marriage must be in at least some difficult cases.

The official Chinese response to the increase in divorces and the presence of "third person interference" is interesting, as it reflects the partially hidden Chinese sense of racial superiority. This "loose morality" is claimed to be an unfortunate import from the West, a result of the increased "spiritual pollution" of contact with the outside world. In the behind-the-scenes struggle over the adoption of Western ways in China those advocating Western business and economic methods seem to be winning at the moment, while it is on the moral front that there seems to be a hidden sense that the foreigners are bad and wrong. To us it seemed amazing that even the most intelligent of our students had difficulty coping with the obvious fact that it is a changing China, particularly one in which women are less willing to be treated as chattels obedient to their husband's wishes, which is the real cause of social change. If the West with its high marriage failure rates offers a model for the escape from marriage as drudgery it is just that, a model. For the Chinese woman to follow that model there must be dissatisfaction in her own situation, and even the authorities are admitting, through the support of campaigns in sex education and marriage advice, that young Chinese often marry woefully ignorant of the details of the facts of life. The general Chinese view of married life, like that which wowed naive MS magazine back page columnist Marcia Yudkin (MS Feb., 1986) is one of a courtly romanticism almost devoid of sexual drive. Lovers quote favorite Western love poets such as Keats and Byron to one another, their minds apparently unstained with lust until the near-rape which often takes place on the wedding night.

Before we ever heard our chorus of frogs we had already had a dose of the firecracker and Xmas light routine of Shanghai marriage, although our first exposure was so uncertain that I had to check with my students before I knew what we had seen and heard.

Behind our apartment block was one of the new six-story blocks which are sprouting like spring bamboo in the outer areas of the city. This one stood empty for a while after our arrival, a seemingly extraordinary event in a city with 380,000 people waiting for a place so that they can marry. We were told that the delay was caused by the workers who refused to finish until they were promised apartments in the building and, given that we also heard of a Chinese teacher of English who could not get his gas hooked up until he agreed to give English lessons to the gasfitter and his son, we could believe such dealing over something as important as a modern flat. In any event the building finally started to fill and almost every night there were tremendous barrages of firecrackers in the street and strange colored lights exhibited in windows across the way. My students informed me that the firecrackers (the straight BANG type only of a very loud vintage and on the traditional repeating strings) were for good luck when the couple moved in although in fact the practice originally was to scare away devils. One presumes there are no devils in modern China or else the tradition has lost its roots. The lights, we discovered when our cleaning girls expressed surprise at our Christmas preparations, are strings of Western-style Christmas lights which are used to light the marriage bedroom. In the little I know of Chinese customs this does not follow any precedents, so perhaps it is adopted from the rose-tinted hues of the Western romantic vision of the big night.

Before the happy couple get to their many-colored bedroom, they have been players in a game so markedly different from that in the West that it raises deep questions about the assumptions by which we live. Partly to control population and perhaps partly for other reasons such as freeing young minds for study and work, the Chinese have structured a pattern of love and marriage in which no woman expects to marry before twenty-three and where twenty-five is a more likely age. Young men get a bonus in their pay for every year beyond thirty that they stay single, and the whole process retarding marriage is furthered by the fact that one must get permission from one's unit to marry, as marriage will entail financial transfers and the finding of all-important space to live. Plenty of young couples find themselves crammed into a tiny room in their parents' apartment or even sharing a room with a curtain or screen dividing it.

A Western reaction to this situation of late marriage is that it must create immense sexual frustration, "cheating," and probably violence and high levels of deviance. Raised as we are on Freud, whether explicitly or implicitly, we cannot easily imagine a society in which so-called "natural drives" do not dominate sexual development. But the Chinese seem to have disregarded such "natural drives" and set up a pattern of society which is different.

This large difference shows itself in many small and fascinating ways. My undergraduate students, who are turning twenty, show no obvious interest in the opposite sex. They arrange themselves in classrooms with seatmates of the same sex. Outside classes they group in the same ways, although there is no real prohibition on mixing. In this aspect they behave like thirteen-year old Americans, but of course they are far more mature intellectually and in other ways. These young men and women, and even graduate students in their late twenties, hold hands and put their arms around members of their own sex freely and openly. While it would be naive to assume that there is no homosexual-lesbian love in China, it was certainly the impression of all the Westerners with whom

I discussed this that the same sex contact was essentially friendship. Nor does it seem, and who can know another's reasons (particularly across cultures and languages), that this was an outlet for "repression" of normal sexual natures.

Complicating the image of this society which simply refutes Western understanding of sex and love is the overlay of confused information from Western culture which appears in strange ways in the realms of sex and love in China. At a Christmas party for the foreign experts a group of young girls did a demonstration of modern dance which was eerie in the way the movements, laden with sexual implication, were performed wholly without understanding. The same appeared in the Chinese fascination with Western dancing which, besides being five or ten years out of date, consisted in young people at student parties and elsewhere doing dances whose meaning they quite clearly did not understand. This same shift of understanding hit home one day as, driving with the very slow traffic on a summer day on the Nanjing Lu, we saw a pretty young girl in a graceful fullskirted silken dress lift the hem to wipe the sweat from her face, placing her full front on display. This gesture, unconscious as it was, was the mark of something so very different from the modesties of our customs. Yet the skittish response of our students to generalized questions about love and marriage both confirmed the importance of these matters, the students' immaturity in dealing with them (by Western standards of age and behavior) and the overwhelming idealism and romanticism that images love and marriage for Chinese youth.

This approved model of marriage for love, society, and children with sex on the side shares with its Victorian counterpart a dark side, although it would be very difficult to gauge its effect and size. Sexual intercourse before marriage *with* the consent of both parties is rape if the parents object, and is punished with serious prison sentence for the man. For the woman, the shame is enough. A quite current Chinese short story which I read in translation involved a rape without consent and, to my horror, the girl drowned herself in shame. We heard of an English teacher who had promised to marry a Chinese student, presumably slept with her, and then excused himself and left China. The probable outcome of this thoughtless act will be that the girl will forever remain unmarried, as do most widows and divorcees in China, although remarriage is becoming an issue in contemporary plays and fiction.

A final and very real difficulty, and one which has a more than slight echo in our society, is the difficulty for educated women in finding husbands who are willing to share careers and childraising. My female graduate students raised this issue when I was asking about marriage practices and the men in the group (12 men and 3 women) responded with the giggles which mean either embarrassment or humor (and hence are so difficult to interpret) and with a number of statements about women's place which would put North American chauvinists to shame.

Yet all of these differences in age and attitude and understanding leave something of the core of love and marriage in place. We were honored by one of our friends at our Institute with an invitation to his wedding, and arrived at a hotel to dine and toast and make merry. The bride was beautiful, the groom happy, embarrassed, and wearing the traditional make-up rouge, the food was amazing, and there was the scene which must be unique to Chinese marriages: not only were two very much extended families in attendance but all of the major figures from the Institute and, presumably, from the bride's work unit who are so much a part of the couple's life. The wedding cars would have come from them and much of the arranging of the feast as well. And, typical of any wedding, there were some young men who got slightly drunk (and presumably ribald) and there were, several weeks later, wedding pictures and honeymoon pictures from a trip to a far part of the country. The only custom which stood out from a Western wedding was that of the bride lighting cigarettes for the groom's parents and later for the other guests. For me this courteous and graceful gesture combined the pleasant idea of being already received as new hostess with the less-pleasant echo of a wife subservient to her husband and in-laws, but that was only more grist for my mill in trying to understand Chinese love and marriage.

I come away from this subject reflecting just how extraordinary and strange *our* styles must seem to the Chinese. Our women don't cover their shoulders, everyone rushes about from the age of twelve (or is it younger?) seeking love and sex, and we are preoccupied with sex in our advertising, our fashions, our self-confidence and the innuendos that pepper our speech. In no area could foreigners be more foreign to the Chinese and it would not surprise me in the least if the Chinese also think of frogs when they are trying to figure out the weird customs of the strangers from outside of the middle kingdom.

Myths

If you've never been in Shanghai and if your images
of it are based on the Western images of modern China as
ours were there are plenty of surprises about the way things
really are. To resident visitors with time to sit chatting over
cups of hong cha (red tea, called black tea in the West) or liu
cha (green or China tea) the bits and pieces of what happens
and what is seen gradually fall together into what seems to be
explanations and understanding. I say "seems" because of the
extraordinary difficulty of ever being certain in the press and
rush of the city. But the myths which are dispelled and, no
doubt, some that are created, give those on the spot a sense
of better understanding Shanghai, and, by extension, something about China today than can come from those who sit
in Hong Kong and gather reports from the tiny flow of dis-
gruntled emigrants from the People's Republic. In this chapter then, I will try to talk about the perceived understanding
which comes from being there, on the condition that my
readers accept what I think about what I see as my own and
that of my fellow foreign teachers, not the conclusions of
experts or surveys.

First among the myths is the overwhelming image of the
Chinese people as all the same, a vast and faceless horde who
think, feel and act together as they have been programmed to
do by a monolithic leadership exerting an iron control from
the cradle onward. Well, beyond the basic fact that almost
everyone is in favor of Chinese socialism (the Chinese do not
yet feel their revolution has progressed far enough to call it
communist) there is a divergence of personalities and opin-

63

ions about everything from the price of rice to the route to progress to fashions and to what Chinese socialism actually is. The rigid education system is rigid mainly in enforcing high levels of study and the presentation and explanation of official Marxism, but no system ever devised could repress the combination of curiosity, reasoning power and individuality which is the Chinese personality. At present Mao Zedong's strong and extreme popular revolutionary stance is in eclipse, although Mao has taken a distinguished place in contemporary Chinese history. Yet we spoke to neo-Maoists who clearly were in doubt about the present policies which are swinging toward new forms of management of capital and the concentrated development of skilled classes of managers and technologists. Within those universities which did not close in the Cultural Revolution there is now tension between a group of leaders and senior teachers who were put in place when academic standards were sacrificed to the adjusted social make-up of the Cultural Revolution and who are now perceived as deadwood oppressing the new, often foreign-trained teachers. While one whole generation of Chinese youth suffered from being snatched from the cities in the Cultural Revolution and being sent to the countryside to work, a different generation who then occupied the educational institutions now finds itself in the crippling position of being, in middle age, a body of wholly unrespected middle-level professionals. They have only the certificates given in place of degrees during the Cultural Revolution and these have lost most of their meaning.

Far from being close-minded about a set of Marxist principles the Chinese are constantly debating the meaning of their political-economic philosophy and its application. There is a vast range of positions presented to the foreigner and there may be even more in debate among the Chinese. Many, such as a young engineer of our acquaintance, are so committed to their work (in her case the design and construction of a tunnel under the Huang Po River at Shanghai) that they do not have any real political commitment. If challenged, they presumably simply point to their work as their contribution. Likewise, students in universities and institutes in Shanghai have political education classes on Friday afternoons but according to reports we received a great deal of sleeping, newspaper reading and knitting gets done. The predominantly rural peasant revolution which culminated in 1949 is reflected in the functionaries of the Party at present, while the intellectuals, including university students, seem relatively uninterested and unwilling to be part of the political structure in any active fashion. While those Friday afternoons are useful for explanations of current changes of official policy, students and intellectuals alike remember the horrors of political involvement in the Cultural Revolution and the Party is having trouble adding to its 40,000,000 members by campaigning among the intellectuals.

Outside of the political shadings are all of the sheer differences of personalities which made our Chinese friends and students so fascinating and such a wonderful pleasure. The engineer spoken of above is 26, with an advanced degree, but with pigtails and laughing eyes she looks eighteen. When it emerges that she is in charge of the design and construction of a major underiver tunnel we are dumbfounded. So, it appears, are the German and British visiting tunnel experts who usually mistake her for a tea girl when she begins to lead the tours of "her" tunnel as it pushes forward several meters a day. Next she will be taking a major hand in the subway about to be built beneath the city.

Then there is our ayi (eye-E), or auntie, the servant offered us by our Institute to help take care of Emma, to cook, to clean and to do our laundry. We don't like the word servant but our hosts insist on using it. Si Ayi is short, broadfaced and usually smiling, a peasant woman from Chongming Island in the Yangtze mouth. She has married an engineering professor in Tongji University and they have two teenaged children, one of whom was taking the important and oft dreaded university entrance examinations while we were in Shanghai. Si loves jokes and comic situations. She has very little English indeed although she is a lightning-quick learner of almost anything. She tolerates difficulties pleasing Emma, who sees herself at 4½ as having only one very definite mother, and lives with what she must see as the mad confusions of helping the foreigners. When we get over our half embarrassment at being offered a servant for $30 a month for a six-day week in a socialist country we arrange for Si to do our laundry and at her request produce a washboard and the necessary detergent. Then begins a long and hilariously troubled battle of wits as she washes the living hell out of everything, rubbing fabrics to a pulp with strong and willing arms. Our wardrobes degenerate, a greater problem for me than for the others as there are few basic clothes in my large sizes easily available. So we start doing some of our own laundry on the sly, hiding things from Si. This is tricky to do as she takes absolute possession of our flat. Philosophically I think of this as the fascinating line between socialist equality and Western ways, the servant who has all the rights. In practice Susan and I are far from philosophical, forced instead to try to tell Si without offense that we want to read or work or nap without her presence.

This situation reaches its apex at dinner times. The first dinner Si ever cooks is a banquet on a scale so massive that we must rush out and get a friend who can explain in Chinese that we could not possibly eat it all. In the end the meal is eaten by our family, although Emma, in her supper-hour sulk (named the "arsenic hour" for children in general by our Maryland colleague Bruce Wilson) does not eat much, and by four other people we invite in on the moment. Thereafter Si cooks too much but not so much and then stands to watch us eat it. Try this sometime. You will require a chef who does not speak your language but by looks and gestures (including loading your plate for you) can make you wish to crawl under a stone because you are not eating her mountains of food and she is mightily offended and worried that she is not pleasing you. Si, her heart in entirely the right place, could take the edge off almost any appetite out of sheer kindness.

Also killing with kindness is one of the wai ban assistants who is, quite frankly, as incompetent as Si or our young engineer are effective. He is perhaps the model for what is wrong with a system where a place must be found for everyone. After teachers' college and several years in the Municipal Education Bureau he is foisted on our wai ban and assigned to us. His English is fine most of the time although with those anachronisms that come from text book learning. He compliments Susan for looking "a real swell" when she is dressed up. The difficulty really lies in the fact that he enjoys playing with the language like an abstract toy rather than giving or receiving meaningful statements in it, and our statements are getting more and more forceful until we are using a lot of terms not in any English dictionary without getting what we want at all. While we are used to the phrasing "This is not what we do in China," and we hope that we are being reasonably understanding and willing to compromise for cultural practices, this young assistant fumbler cannot even stop spouting in English or talking about how he is learning the subtleties of the language from us long enough to meet even reasonable requests. We begin to suspect two things. First, despite his obvious generalized desire to please, he seems to have no power, no guanxi, to get things done. He has not known the drivers long enough, he does not know the nurses at the Hua Dong Hospital, he simply has not yet built up the web needed to get action even if he pauses long enough to hear our requests. Second, he is, in any language, not very very bright. This finally comes home to me on a day outing when he is supposed to be taking care of Emma, myself, George, and Holly (two of my fellow teachers). With us also is Professor Li, my superior and a gentleman of great dignity who combines what must have been the courtesy of the old China with the struggles and survival of revolutionary China.

It is when Professor Li begins to become progressively more angry at our fumbler's performance, climaxing when we walk a mile or so on a hot dusty road along which the van could have driven and does drive only *after* we have walked it, that I realize that it is not the strangeness of the foreigner which makes the fumbler seem a fool. He is one.

I could continue indefinitely to catalogue the nearly infinite variety of the Chinese we meet, from the helpful doctors at the Hua Dong Hospital with their curiosity about Western hospitals and their drafting of foreign patients as interpreters of medical articles, to the cleverest student I have ever taught anywhere, to the fu wu yuan, our flighty, casual, singing housecleaning girls (who horrified Si Ai to anger sometimes by the careless swipe they would often give to our apartment floors) who flitted through our flat six days a week and arranged momentous matters such as selling us that strange commodity—toilet paper. The myth that "they're all the same" would be funny except that it may be believed. In fact people go about their lives in their way in China no more notably bound by the political process than citizens of any other country. In some ways the very fact that nearly every citizen of Shanghai has a base of security liberates the individual to show his or her quirks, although the net of guanxi balances this with the need to present oneself as at least acceptable to many of one's own friends and contacts.

Another myth, although one which North American experience prepares us to doubt, is that all Chinese, with the possible exception of a few party leaders, are equal. Certainly, from being a stratified semi-feudal nation of exceptional class rigidity in the late nineteenth century, socialist China has achieved a remarkable leveling evidenced in such basic matters as eating and a place to sleep. At first the mixture of ordinary blue and gray clothing and frequent flashes of Western dress seem to give very little indication of rank and position and language prevents the foreigner from judging clearly whether conversations are discussions, arguments, chastisements or the issuing of orders. Gradually, however, a clear pecking order begins to emerge. First comes the realization that hotels and other establishments catering to foreign guests have only selected Chinese customers. These may be army officers or businessmen or tour couriers or officials in from the countryside for meetings or negotiations. Other Chinese are stopped at the doors of such establishments. Then one notices the "two pen cadres," officials dressed in the formal gray or blue Mao jackets (which are actually named in China for Zhong Shan—Sun Yat Sen—who popularized the style) and with several pens clipped in the pocket. This, along with the cut of the garment, identifies the rank of the wearer. These jackets can be bought in any local department store but they tend to fit poorly. When they fit well, however, it is because a skilled tailor has been at work. It is part of Shanghai's reputation that the Beijing leaders come here for their tailoring as well as calling on Shanghai's doctors for their health. So the well-tailored Mao jacket with pens marks off rank and prestige just as the quality custom suit does in the West.

When it comes to Western dress, however, the Chinese are not apt at expressing rank. With the exception of one Paris-educated official from the Municipal Government of Shanghai who was a guest of honor at our introductory banquet, I saw no one in an elegantly-tailored Western-style suit. Occasional run-ins with oddities in Chinese custom tailoring such as a shirt pocket which sneaked around to shelter in my armpit and a cashmere coat made for an Australian friend of ours that came out looking like "a large brown toilet roll" suggest that standards in Western dress tend to be pretty vague. But the Mao jacket provides a subtle yet clear mark of prestige and they can be exceptionally elegant if one has the right tailor. That same tailor can even achieve elegance using the heavy winter cloth and lining out of which the winter versions of the garment are cut.

Socialist inequality also comes out in the question of town and country. Although one distinct impression of

Shanghai, prompted by the lined and darkened faces and simplicities of style of life, is that the Revolution has made the peasants dominant in city life, there is in fact a considerable arrogance in the city dweller toward the peasants. This gulf between the 700,000,000 in the countryside and their city cousins is complicated by the ideals of the Revolution which place the peasant at the center and by the fact that almost everyone has plenty of country cousins or has even come into Shanghai in his lifetime. It is proper to admire the peasants but I noticed a consistent lumping of them into a vast grouping with implications that my young intellectuals were going to manage them. It was probably this accidental arrogance of the rulers from the city, so like the attitude of the landlord class that the Revolution had destroyed, which prompted Mao to disrupt the society with the Cultural Revolution. The net result of that upheaval on the attitudes in the city is very strange, if my graduate students and the university teachers we met, almost all returned from the countryside, are to serve as a test. They still have mixed feelings toward the peasants, prompted perhaps by the fact that they were persecuted as fools when they tried to survive outside the city in the hardships and misery of a peasant life of arduous manual labor and yet they were often helped to survive by those same persecutors. As a future generation of China's leaders and managers they will never be able to forget the hardness and the kindness of the peasants alongside whom they struggled and sweated for their survival when they were sent down. What that will mean for the future of China, even if it is presently the popular view that the Cultural Revolution was a disaster, will undoubtedly be of the greatest importance. Yet there lingers a powerful sense that to be poor but to be in Shanghai makes one superior to being rich in the country.

One final myth about China is that it has a vast standing army and imperialist intentions. It no doubt has many men in uniform but all that amateurs like ourselves could determine suggests that they are seen almost solely as self defense forces if one allows for the fact that China has historically viewed its self defense as including the absence of hostile countries and influences in the countries on its borders. In Shanghai, as opposed to areas of the country such as the Soviet frontier and major military installations, one is struck by the fact that the army is not standing but walking and working. To this Canadian author traveling into the United States is always a surprise because of the number of men in uniform traveling through airports whereas the small Canadian military travels in mufti. In Shanghai the army rides the busses and works on a vast variety of construction and other useful jobs. While China's army may be powerful the urban soldiers are very informal and their illfitting green uniforms and running shoes of various shades make one aware of the reality of a "Peoples' Army" which is a very active agent *in* its society rather than distanced from it and held inside a rigid grouping of camps and bases where it eats and lives at public expense.

Our twelve-year-old son, Mike, and his British companion, Jack, ventured onto an army base on their bicycles one afternoon. They later swore it was "by accident" and that the large sign (which, surprisingly, was in English as well as Chinese) was rusty and they missed it. In any event they and their bicycles were seized and they spent a bit over an hour at the guardhouse being harangued and questioned. Jack, who had a lot more workable Chinese than Mike, did not try too hard to understand, I gather, and eventually, after threats of having their bicycles confiscated, they were released and sent packing. They were probably correctly viewed as slight risks to Chinese national security and may have been of more interest to their captors because very few twelve-year-old Chinese children own bicycles and they may have been suspected of theft more than military intelligence. Bicycles are most noticeably not toys in Shanghai. Our experience of the army varied from this incident on the one hand to very gentlemanly and frequently aged senior officers who attended the civic reception for the thirty-fifth anniversary of the Revolution. These senior officers, presumably of the Shanghai garrison, were clad in immaculate uniforms and were much decorated. Even if the "vast standing army" is in fact clad in tennis shoes and doing the peoples' business in Shanghai, that view of its leaders did serve to remind us that it has a direct influence on the state it was instrumental in creating.

Much That Is New Is Old

China, a country which has seen an almost unparalleled upheaval and change in the twentieth century, should be a country in which everything is new and different. Except for a few monuments, temples, the Wall and the Grand Canal—the physical remains—everything should be the product of the thought and process of social, economic, and political change which has now had generations to complete its remaking of a people. And this is what strikes you as you step off a plane in Shanghai in the dusk and walk through workers with jackhammers under arc' lights finishing the new airport. And it is what strikes you in the spirit of the people, committed to the new and looking forward.

But the longer you look at people and processes and things in Shanghai the more you begin to see that the new is the old, or very like the old in many ways. What little I had read of old China, and what I could find out by reading classical fiction in translation while snuggled under the down comforter, good Chinese beer to hand, in the long winter evenings, suggests that the struggle to make anew is really a struggle for compromises, that such an ancient and mighty civilization has deep roots and leaves great gouging marks in any highway of progress that tries to pass over it.

For me the most immediate realization came from the way in which teaching and learning take place in a Chinese Institute or University. The classroom, probably familiar to readers from photographs, features desks with bench seats for students seated in twos and a wooden dias platform about six inches high across the front with its high lectern-desk for the teacher. The psychological implications of this system are clear, and descriptions of such a schoolroom and the teaching in it figure in *The Dream of the Red Chamber,* an eighteenth century classic novel. In the room the teacher stands above the student, accorded respect for the learning he presumably has. Students in Chinese classes are expected to listen quietly and with respect. They do not challenge the teacher and they rarely ask questions. In these respects little or nothing has changed in the system of Chinese education and there is still a dreaded and difficult examination system which students must pass.

What has changed, of course, is the social profile of the successful students. With a broad base of public literacy and testing based on the sciences and mathematics as well as the language and the classics many of the new Chinese students are representatives of talent rather than influence or privilege, always given that in any society the literate and learned do give their children the advantage of a love of learning and parental encouragement.

But the vestiges of the old are very powerful. There is still a pride in handling the ink brush, in actually writing well. There remains the deference to the teachers which is embarrassing for foreigners and there remains that marvelous boost for the egos of foreign teachers of being respected and obviously appreciated. To be learned, even in the new China, is not to be foolish, an "egghead" excluded from the real life of society. Rather, one feels appreciated in the most extraordinary fashion, placed as someone who has a valuable gift which they are giving; knowledge. And this too has its antecedents, for teachers, usually called by the preface Lao, (translated into English as venerable or honorable) have always had such honor in China and have long held the means of entry into the official classes and positions of power. For teachers have traditionally had a stranglehold on knowledge itself due to the difficulty of typing Chinese ideographs. This has kept printed books to a minimum until most recent times so that scholars who have libraries have passed knowledge to students personally. In Shanghai today libraries are strictly controlled and students' access to books is extremely difficult. In essence they still depend upon the teacher as the font of knowledge which of course breeds respect and careful treatment.

The kindness toward teachers is also part of the Chinese attitudes of consideration for people which are rooted in the past yet carry through to today. After every journey or lecture or other activity, both students and staff urge teachers to rest, drink or eat. I was always being instructed to sit down, to rest, to take tea and I was always being asked, with great concern, "Have you eaten?" (One has to be very careful of this question, as it is one of the oldest forms of polite greeting in most of China, and may not quite mean what it says.) Besides the obvious compliment that I and other foreigners were being cared for so carefully and must be of value, it appears that this care is a reflection of the way in which the Chinese have always paid attention to routines of food and rest as a major component of health. *The Dream of the Red Chamber* is full of careful descriptions of special foods which people send as gifts to each other for specific purposes. Chinese who could afford care in the past rested with great regularity and ate with great regularity and the Chinese of today still do so. Shanghai stops quite dead for lunch at 1130 hours and follows this with a xiu xi, about an hour of sleep or rest. This rest of course makes great sense in the heat of the Chinese summer but it is not a habit which any Shanghai winter will ever put a stop to.

Much has been written lately about Chinese traditional medicine and its effects have been vouched for not only by the Chinese people but by foreigners who were treated in Shanghai. In fact one of my graduate students, a statistician, had spent his year previous to graduate studies setting up statistical testing programs for the Shanghai Traditional Medicine College, to aid in research and offer Westerners their own

traditional reassurance of the efficacy of the treatments—
statistics.

What it seems important to add is that the actual medical
treatment is only a part of an attitude towards health which
includes great emphasis on diet, rest and moderation. In
Shanghai and other Chinese areas which swelter in great heat
and high humidity for part of the year people still do not
consume ice cold drinks because these have always been considered to be foreign to the human constitution and therefore
liable to break the balance of nature and possibly bring on
illness. Even foreigners often encounter a genuine reluctance
to serve them cold drinks (because, of course, what is good
for oneself is good for one's guests) and to get a cold beer in
a hotel in Wuxi we were told that we would have to place the
order at breakfast in order to get it for supper. Thirsty and
impatient, we settled for warm beer with our dinners to the
obvious satisfaction of the solicitous waiters who undoubtedly felt that they had won another battle in the constant
struggle to keep the foreign fools healthy. When I came down
with pneumonia and spent a week in the hospital another aspect of traditional Chinese attitudes toward health became
obvious. After excellent and straightforward Western style
medicine in the Hua Dong Hospital everyone, my Institute's
leaders and the doctors, advised a long rest at my home, a
minimum of three weeks, to recover and build up my strength.
I did quite a bit of arguing about this, as I felt obligations to
my students and I have had pneumonia before as an adult
and know something of recovering from it. I did manage to
reduce my recuperation by one week but I should have real-
ized that from my hosts' points of view I was being very foolish. I was ill at the beginning of the Winter and to the Chinese
this has traditionally been the worst time of year to become
ill. It is the season when the lack of fresh vegetables and fruits
and the lack of central heat (although there is now central
heating throughout much of Northern China and in earlier
times there were heated kangs or sleeping platforms for those

76

who could afford them) make recovery enormously difficult and those falling ill near the end of the year usually received the prognosis that if they lived through the cold they would survive and were treated with all of the sorts of care and rest I was being given in 1985. For these traditions have not died, and in the cases of my Chinese colleagues, their wisdom has not died either. It is only the foreigner, with his unusual luxuries of a higher energy diet than the average Shanghai citizen and the comfort of central heating, who is in a position to count on a rapid recovery in the Shanghai winter.

At the very center of the modern Chinese state is the concept of the "unit" or danwei. In the countryside the Party and the Army organized village units, which at the height of the early reforms in agriculture were the communes, a system in which everyone worked on common lands and shared services. Since the more recent reforms of 1978 the units have been renamed village committees and they have taken in hand the various aspects of the privatization of agriculture and experiments in land management which are a part of efforts to improve agricultural production (this appears to be very successful) and to move excess manpower to rural manufacturing roles.

In Shanghai, however, the growth of the unit system was different and more gradual but the units are now the central fact of everyone's life. A child is initially attached to the unit of his parents, preference being given to the mother's unit but other factors, such as which unit is providing a room or apartment, may figure in this. The child remains in this unit until he or she goes to post-secondary education and from the unit of College or University he moves to his workplace unit. If units do not provide their own housing they make rental arrangements with other units for their members who must be housed.

Within each unit there is a bureaucratic structure which sees to the distribution of just about everything from health care and food to work itself, including the community work which most people do one-half day every two weeks on things like gardening or maintenance. The unit also carries its own elderly members, often placing them in useful tasks such as minding children and tending the innumerable gatehouses. The intricate structure of the unit is the functioning microcosm of the Chinese political system, the delivery point of services and information and political instruction and directives. It is applied socialism, handling the problem of who shall have the four automobiles available to, say, 600 people in a given day and trying to take into account the needs of leaders, the needs of those getting married and the needs for running errands to a supplier or collecting the large cash payroll (everyone is paid in wads of banknotes) at the Bank of China. It is the level at which health care is delivered through clinics and the equation of how much care can be given to everyone is weighed against the needs of a particular person for special care. It is the level at which many personal disputes and difficulties are resolved, often without consulting higher officials.

What is old about the unit is that it replicates the large families of older China, clans which included three or four generations of several families and vast armies of servitors and others in positions to be essentially taken care of under a sort of *noblesse oblige.* The new units are of course radically different in their structure and distribution of power from their feudal antecedents, but they provide the same sort of all-embracing control and authority over the lives of those within them. They tacitly admit that structures offering security are wanted by the people, and that the connection to others in large groups who provide mutual help is very much the Chinese way.

We actually experience the danwei or unit at work in Shanghai in a vast number of minor ways, for although we are attached to the work unit of our Institute and carry the card in its red plastic folder which identifies us as such we are of course foreign guests rather than fully active participants

78

in our unit. I discover that the car which takes me to work each morning has just come from a previous run which brings the president of the 2,500-student Institute to his work. I likewise discover that I cannot arbitrarily dictate when I want the car or the Institute van to take me back to my home because it may be at other tasks or the drivers may be taking their xiu xi or servicing their vehicles.

Besides paying our salaries the unit is entwined in many other aspects of our lives. At the Institute there are cafeterias where we eat lunch, using very inexpensive meal tickets which can be bought only by members of the Institute's unit, and our apartment was arranged and provided by the unit. In fact, our living arrangements offer us a short introductory course in unit to unit contact since we are living in housing our unit is renting from another. Where we live we see the domestic aspects of the unit. In our foreigners' apartment building all of the work is done by members of the Tongji University unit which operates the building for its foreign teachers. The girls who clean our house, the gatekeepers, the kitchen staff, Ayi, the handyman-engineer who fixes electrical systems and drains, the staff who stoke a coal-fired steam plant which provides us with hot water and even our Si are drawn from the larger unit, which in turn feeds and cares for them. The gardening, and we boast a lawn as well as amazing roses and a variety of sub-tropical trees (Shanghai has conifers next to palms, roses cohabiting with small but fruitful banana trees), is managed by several career gardeners but students, as part of the university unit, give their half-day every two weeks to weeding or other assistance and waves of happy, chatting housewives also move slowly across the lawns on tiny stools, pulling the weeds from the grass, trimming it with scissors (we saw no lawnmower), and stopping willingly to chat with Emma or the other foreign children. In the apartment buildings around ours the unit operates in full swing and includes a modest shopping district, a noodle shop where grains are also sold, the nursery schools and secondary school, a bakery (unlike other foreigners inland in China we get white and rye bread easily), an assembly hall, several small but busy playing fields, and a street medical clinic. The unit has a full-time tai chi chuan teacher who gave the foreigners a course in the tennis court near our building but could be seen at other hours working with two or three old people or a group of housewives in a small park.

There seems to be a considerable emphasis on the independence of the individual units. Foreign teachers often come up against this when photocopiers or video machines break down and it is discovered that one's unit has a technician but that there are no central repair services for goods. If your own man can't cope, and this becomes problematic as more advanced technologies come into use, then it may take a very long time to get machines operating. This may also be related to the fact that going outside the unit requires hard money, where staying in it only uses a member's time, which is always at the disposal of the unit anyway.

In the extended community families of old China one of the great difficulties of human life, particularly for the young, was that the patriarch or matriarch of the family frequently chose the careers for the junior members without consultation. One was effectively stymied from striking off on one's own by the need for connections and introductions to other families needed in order to build a future. In China today the unit vastly complicates the situation because it often acts in the role of the family head while at the same time family patterns continue to co-exist with it. University students are part of their university units and many of them in this generation find themselves pressed to fill the roles of teachers even if they wish to go out and apply their learning. Many of the best are drawn off to stay within their unit to help fill the gaps created by the loss of the previous generation of young intellectuals to the Cultural Revolution. Those who do go elsewhere are placed by their unit with minimal consultation, and the results are occasionally painful because the family-dependent Shanghai student suddenly discovers that he or she has been placed in a business or teaching post in another city. It is a tribute to the traditions of respecting others' decisions for oneself that most of these assignments are obeyed and it speaks well for such traditions that in frequent cases the intelligence of those in the unit placing the students makes few mistakes and helps to effectively exploit the available educated manpower.

Walls are another distinctive part of the old China which carry over into the present day. In ancient China there was a three-wall system; one ringing the outer city including the immediately surrounding farmlands, one ringing the city proper and individual walls ringing the compound of each family. Once the family compound was shut at night it was a very private place, a small universe of matriarch and patriarch ruling over their married children, their grandchildren, miscellaneous minor relatives, a tutor perhaps, and a vast array of servants. In the daytime gates were opened although the main gate was frequently kept shut except for ceremonial entrances and exits of family members or their guests. There have always been gatehouses and gatemen, exerting control over who enters and perhaps physically opening and closing the gates.

This system of small islands has not really changed in Shanghai today excepting perhaps in the design of the vast apartment developments in the north and south of the city. The compound consisting of our two foreigners' apartment buildings, the lawns surrounding them, the tennis court, the bicycle shed and the small children's playground are enclosed by a mixture of walls and hedges and the road entrance is marked by a large gate and gatehouse. But this is not merely the case for foreigners. Our compound is inside the grounds of the Tongji University unit and it too has gates and a wall. So do the universities and colleges we work at or visit and so do hotels like the Jin Jiang which have surrounding grounds. A new factory which was being built near us was being surrounded by its wall even as it was under construction, as was the satellite campus of our Institute, where the guardians of the gate were temporarily under canvas until their gatehouse could be constructed.

A Westerner's initial reaction to these arrangements may be to see them as some sort of Communist repression, of state control, and certainly some of the press reports coming from foreign correspondents in China stress the sense of being isolated. I understand that in Beijing there actually is a foreigner's section of the city and as few reporters seem to do much work outside the capital it would not be surprising if they saw themselves as walled in. But it is clearly a practice which has far deeper roots and is, in the end, a part of the Chinese social fabric, an expression of the social closeness and mutual assistance among groups of people in one of the oldest civilizations in the world.

Another side of the old China which persists into the new is the separation between town and country. My students who had been sent to the countryside during the Cultural Revolution had a grudging respect for the peasants and particular fond memories of individuals who helped them through those hard times. In the end, however, they clearly felt that there could be nothing worse than having to grow up and live in the country and their efforts to return to Shanghai were many and varied according to where they had been sent. In several cases the pattern had been from field laborer to offering night classes to fellow workers to village teacher to town teacher to a teacher in a technical college and finally through entrance exams to a place in an Institute in Shanghai. One young woman told me about learning English while absolutely isolated from anyone else doing the same thing by working with a textbook after days in the fields and listening, on occasion, to English radio broadcasts. All of this effort and devotion centered around getting back to the beloved city and away from the country. This lack of a parallel to the "back to the land" pastoral tradition of Western countries seems to exist for two main reasons. First, in the ancient China of the empire all power lay in the court, so much of China's great writing idolizes the city at the expense of the country. Second, life in the countryside of China has always been exceptionally hard in the face of crowding, flood and storm. Many of the areas not open to foreigners today are not military zones or the sites of horrible secrets but simply places where there are not yet any living facilities which the Chinese consider adequate for their foreign guests. In light of such harsh conditions there is little wonder that the city dwellers wish to stay where they are. In Shanghai this is usually stated in terms of the availability of restaurants, books, cinemas, friends and easy accessibility to new televisions or the best bicycles. The true revolutionary undercurrent in Shanghai in 1985 is the dawning realization and accompanying envy that countryside workers are earning more than city workers since the agricultural reforms of 1978. This is indicated by a continuing stream of complaints about wage differentials and such stories as that of a successful farmer who is reputed to have added a two-car garage to his new house at a time when there are few private automobiles in China. These reforms seem to reinforce the official preeminence of the peasant in modern China, which is a true reversal of ancient forms, and it was interesting to note that the Chinese television we watched never had a comic peasant character although there were plenty of parodies of scholars, some of businessmen, and many of the old styles of state official.

One way in which the Chinese have clearly not changed at all is in their perspective on the rest of the world. In his marvelous book, *Chinese Looking Glass*, Dennis Bloodworth tells of the arrival in 1793 of an emissary from George the Third, then ruler of an Empire much larger than China and still growing in glory. That emissary, "Our Well-Beloved Cousin and Counsellor, the Right Honourable George Lord Viscount Macartney" (with many more titles following) was looked over at his port of arrival and sent forward to Peking with a banner flying over his boat on which was written "Tribute Embassy from the Red Barbarians." The Emperor did entertain Marcartney to breakfast but that was just about all he got from several futile months in the capital.

This essential establishment of the meaning of everything and its importance based on what it means to themselves remains a very Chinese characteristic today. You can get really nice French-fried potatoes in Shanghai, a city where deep frying is a lynchpin in the culinary art, but you must expect them to arrive at your table bathed in sugar. Salt would be a ridiculous option, because that is not how it is done in China. This same attitude shows through in the Chinese attitude to popular dancing, where we discovered that the way a Western dance is being done in Shanghai is the way it *should* be done, even if, in fact, it has never been done that way in the country it is copied from. My students who could not separate plagiarism from cooperative work, even after the difference had been frequently explained to them, were victims of the same special focus. If it is not the way the Chinese see things, if it is not converted into a Chinese perspective, then it is not right.

We were taken on a tour of the Shanghai Dubbing Studios, where Western films are dubbed by very skilled actors and technicians. As a treat at the close of our visit we were shown a popular American film just dubbed for distribution in China. It was *First Blood*, the initial Rambo film, and it was introduced to us as "the reaction of an average American soldier on his return home from Vietnam." Fortunately I could not follow the subtitles in Chinese but I shudder to think of how they are likely to carry forward this vision of Rambo as an average American soldier.

After bathing in blood with Sylvester, I gave considerable thought to just what is going on here. Was I watching a propaganda process run by devious minds or was this the application of some undefined, unconsidered way of looking at the barbarians? Certainly we give the Chinese plenty to work with if they wish to see the bad side of Western culture. In answer to questions I later asked, it was pointed out to me that the studio selects the films it will dub, usually on the basis of their popularity in the West.

But what an image this presents, particularly when you remember that the Chinese people see very few foreign films or television shows. They lack the sense of proportion and arrangement which we get from living *in* our world; they are spectators to a vast and confusing dumb show. Not only was *First Blood* about to go on display when we were in China but among the favorite foreign films was *Kramer vs. Kramer*. Consider, as I ruefully did, just what understanding of North American domestic life you would get if you saw only *Kramer vs. Kramer*. It is not in the Chinese modern tradition of art to be critical of the society but rather to support it and show the system positively. So the West provides all of its best-selling art, critical of social institutions or revealing corruption within them (Arthur Hailey is a favorite in China with his heavily romanticized and over-dramatized "pictures" of hotels and airports) and the Chinese largely interpret these as accurate portraits of corrupt societies which they are happy to have no part of. For they start out with the sense that the "Red Barbarians" are out there and they are hardly surprised when we send them our most popular films and books to prove that, because we are not Chinese, we most certainly are barbarians in a wide variety of ways.

I saw another facet of this special superiority complex which descends from the Celestial Empire when an American computer engineer, a software designer, came to China to teach a short course. He was surprised, almost stunned, when the Chinese explained that they wanted to know the range of American softwares not primarily to select what they needed, although they fully intended to do so, but to permit them to select the areas in which they expect to design softwares to sell to the rest of the world in a few years. The rest of the world's computer industry is clearly of interest to the

Chinese because it will provide them with a market when they choose. Everything starts from China. The surprise in all of this was that after three weeks of teaching one of Tom's students did in fact crack a previously unsolved puzzle in software planning, hinting that the dream and the reality may indeed be in touch.

Everyone sees the world through his own experience, and it could be argued that the Chinese are no different from any other race in this way. But there is a strong feeling that ages of civilization and isolation have made them exceptional and that to understand the world from their perspective, the prerequisite to real friendship and mutual concessions, you must grasp this powerfully ethnocentric way of looking at the world.

One hears over and over, whether discovering that there are no round-trip tickets for trains and planes or learning that you cannot select your textbooks by browsing through the half-secret third floor of the Foreign Languages Bookstore where pirated Western texts are sold for students to use in your classroom, the remark "That is not how we do things in China" or the variant "That is not our custom in China." At first that seems a simple statement of a difficulty or a cultural difference but eventually you realize that implicit in it is the critical idea that if "we" do not do things this way they are not worth doing. And, it should not come as any surprise by this point, if "we" do not do things that way in China, there is absolutely no chance that we are going to do them that way because you have asked. I can think of no country in the world, with the possible exception of France, which is so certain so often that its habits and its practices are right. The modernizing governments seek new ways in the new China, but as my students repeatedly told me they intend to select only those ways which are suitable for China. The rest, whether they are computer softwares, cold drinks or modern accounting methods, will not impress the Chinese in the least.

Of all of the old ways which endure into the new China the most complex, fascinating and difficult to explain is *guanxi*, and it is also the wellspring of the structure of the whole Chinese society and the cause for so much of the puzzlement which the stranger feels in the Middle Kingdom. A starting point for this multifaceted and even self-contradictory concept is the precept, derived from Confucius, that even an official must serve his family before the Emperor. Guanxi has a multitude of different translations into English, but the chief among them are relationship, influence, web and net. It is the principle for the movement of power, for getting things done or preventing them from getting done, at once the social cement in China and the concrete walls which often prevent progress or originality.

In its most positive aspects the operation of a vast social net beginning with family, fellow townsmen, fellow students or colleagues permits things to get done because there is established trust of others based on experience and the exchange of help. To get a train ticket you contact your cousin who works for the railway. To arrange an apartment for foreign visitors you contact your colleagues at a university where you used to work and which has an apartment building at its disposal. When something is needed you think of the persons you know who might have access to it and then you ask for their help.

On exposure to this way of doing things the Westerner naively responds with remarks about "influence" and "pull," comparing the practice to the "I can get it for you cheap" or "He has a brother in the government" mentality which is considered unjust and often illegal in the West. "Where," he asks, "is the morality of a society which does this all the time?" In fact, the answer lies right in front of him. This *is* the morality of China, neither unconsidered, vague or "wrong" in any absolute sense once it is understood. Perhaps it is its very resemblance to Western practices which makes it difficult to look at it with an objectivity.

In the turbulent and violent history of China, the mainstay for survival has long been those large extended families living within the walls of their family compound. In this secure net of relationships were clearly fixed, immensely complex structures of indebtedness, fixed by degree so that, for example, a first wife who bore no male issue might be displaced by a concubine who did. Sons owed absolute allegiance to their parents and wives to their husbands. But in exchange for this, and exchange is the key to understanding guanxi, those to whom one owed allegiance were responsible for one. This complex and interlocking network of alliances and mutual interdependence, this spider's web which touched everywhere reverberates back and around to affect other contacts, begins with the family but expands outward to friends and associates, so that every individual is enmeshed in many different nets. But enmeshed and nets must not be seen as traps but rather the way things are meant to be. If everyone in a society understands and practices even so complex a way of making friends, doing business and fulfilling needs, then it is the moral structure of the society.

Nevertheless, the system is vastly confusing and frustrating to foreigners because they are not Chinese and are therefore really not suited to practice it or understand it. If you are not born in a Chinese family you do not have a starting place in the net nor do you learn the intricate ways in which it works. For you cannot just ask anyone you know for anything within this system but must avoid asking for anything more than your invisible "credit" will bear. Moreover, the seemingly quick and easy way of asking for something is notably slowed because every time you tweak the web you commit yourself to offer some return at some indefinite future moment and you affect the "face" or dignity which you have within your relationship. So there is a built-in conservatism, a tendancy to take great care that what you ask for you really need and is really possible.

Almost all of this careful judgment and its operation is beyond the comprehension of anyone who, like ourselves, spends a year in China. But we see fragments of what is happening and speculate on how guanxi is affecting us and those we know. I notice, to begin with, just how friendly and cooperative with each other all of the students in my classes are and how they never openly criticize one another. This, of course, is because Chinese students are sharing with their classmates, with whom they often spend several years since university classes remain intact, the beginning of the formation of the guanxi of their professional group. They reasonably expect that in future years they will be dealing with each other, exchanging acts of guanxi and basing their relationship on their time together as students. It will help them later if they are friendly now and it could certainly hinder and embarrass them if they had to go to someone they knew but had poor relations with. We heard of a party of our fellow teachers who appeared to be stranded in a tourist city because all of the flights out were booked full. Then the wai ban official escorting them discovered one of his former university classmates working as a manager in the airlines office. Then seats were magically found and everyone went on their way.

It took every ounce of my years of experience as a university teacher to finally convince my graduate class to do seminars, in which one student presents and others offer criticism, advice and comments. It was only when we had been together long enough for me to fully explain that it was part of the Western university process to join in mutual criticism in the presence of the professor and until the class were thoroughly used to one another that I was able to introduce seminars. Once begun, they proved immensely popular and revealed the vast variety of judgments and opinions among these intelligent young Chinese students. It is a serious mistake to underestimate the caution which the Chinese show with their friends and fellow students and on reflection it suggests how traumatic the public criticisms and personal self-criticisms which were at the center of the Cultural Revolution and are still occasionally used must be for the Chinese. They comprise a baring of the personality and a stripping away of guanxi masks which must challenge the society's and the individual's solidity.

The student-teacher relationship is another point at which guanxi is apparent. In classical China and in modern China the student is exceptionally respectful while studying with a teacher, accepting the fact that the teacher is his route to position and promotion because, despite the guanxi of family connections, there has always been a premium on learning in China. Western teachers find the students' concern with their teachers' wellbeing almost embarrassingly overwhelming and the respect for the teachers' statements seems to border on the slavish. I say "seems" because I suspect, after some limited successes in a year of trying to get my students to speak out, that they harbor private reservations about much of what they are told and that the real difference between themselves and Western students is that the latter are actually rewarded for arguing and displays of independent thinking. But the degree of formal acquiesence by Chinese students cannot be underrated and I still to this day do not know how serious some of my graduate students were when they threatened?/offered? to perform the traditional ceremony of coming to my home on New Year's Day to kowtow (bow with the forehead touching the floor) to their teacher. What is clear is that the student-teacher relationship does not end at the classroom door but that teachers play a major part in assigning students to their work units and in later years the students often return honors and favors to their former teachers. No group of students I have ever taught have made it so clear to me that I was giving them what they saw as important help and I found myself powerfully drawn to return their appreciation by putting every effort into what I was doing. Teaching in China is only a beginning, for one's students continue to write either for help in finding a book or to report their progress or success and in this continuing connection the foreign teacher can get a tiny glimpse of what the guanxi relationship must be like for the Chinese themselves.

In fact, one of the most difficult things for the foreigner living in China is his ignorance of this system. Much of the frustration one encounters is probably because of a failure to understand that things which are obtained by power or money in the West pose intricate problems for one's Chinese hosts. We saw this when other universities would not reprogram video tapes brought from America to run on the Chinese television system or when we made demands of our institution with regards to problems at our apartment which was in another unit. Efforts would be made to assist us but there was, finally, no way beyond the stock of guanxi available to enforce the will of one unit on another. Besides not knowing just how this process works, or even what relationships were being invoked on our behalf, we often felt suspended, uncertain of whether our unit was trying or had decided it was unable to ask on our behalf. There is no doubt that foreigners are like bulls in china shops when in China, blithely unaware that they are often asking more than is reasonable. This in turn must deeply upset their hosts both because they are embarrassed at not being able to help and because they must see the foreigners as inept and unreasonable even to be asking in the first place. We asked a number of our foreign colleagues with previous experience in China just what guanxi they thought we ourselves had when we came to teach. There is clearly no simple answer to this but it would seem that the Chinese accord some considerable "present" of guanxi to foreigners who come to provide help and there is no doubt that we drew on and overdrew our allocation. But this must be tempered by the unstated fact that the foreigners are not going to live their lives inside the web of guanxi nor will they have much understanding of the relative importance of what they may be asking for. And all of this uncertainty is complicated by the Confucian and Chinese principle of showing the greatest kindness to those one likes the least, presumably because within the Chinese sense of values this engenders a great obligation which the hated ones will never repay, thus placing the Chinese on the highest imaginable moral ground. Once an awareness of all this comes to a foreigner he finds meaning in a vast variety of tiny events and actions, from cars which arrive late to events scheduled when he cannot attend to black weeks when no letters arrive, until a sort of pananoic paralysis may result. Only an awareness that one cannot understand saves one from immobility in the face of the moral jigsaw puzzle of guanxi.

On one occasion we went to a restaurant with Chinese friends and on the way Susan presented a pack of Western cigarettes (the Chinese are keen smokers and have their own vast cigarette industry but Susan says their cigarettes are slightly raw), to our host, partly to pay for having borrowed quite a few. He thanked her and explained it was particularly apropos because he had wanted to obtain some to give to his cousin who, it turned out, was a waitress at the restaurant where we were taken and where we had an exceptional meal. The cigarettes, I understood, ended up in the kitchen, the small but necessary shift of guanxi from the waitress to her colleagues to cover the favor of producing an especially excellent meal.

When difficult requests were put to our hosts and they were in their kindness able to respond, the explanation which came with the tickets, or news of the arrangements, almost inevitably began with the phrase "I have a friend . . . " In one case someone got us the services of a famous tailor because he was the uncle of a classmate. Nor is it unusual to have anyone who knows you urge upon you the addresses of their friends, cousins, uncles or former classmates if they find out that you are going to visit a distant city. To most Westerners this is horribly awkward, for they do not wish to visit total strangers nor do they wish to say so to a Chinese friend who is effusively offering the names. If they were to go they would be welcomed and assisted by the total strangers, their paths to new contacts eased by guanxi and many of the difficulties of new places melted in the Chinese fashion.

In saying that much in the new China is old there is no criticism whatsoever of either the amazing achievements of the Chinese revolutions, climaxed by the Communist Revolution of 1949, nor of the ways themselves as somehow archaic or useless. Rather there is a miracle here, a transformation of much that is wrong in a society without the loss of much that was, and is, good. If an American businessman tears the hairs from his head while waiting three weeks to begin contract negotiations in China, he should be remembering that the Chinese have rarely done business with anyone not connected to them through the web of guanxi and longstanding association. The amazing thing is that his Chinese counterparts may be willing to deal with him at all after only a few weeks of touring, dining and discussions. Nor can anything really be at fault with the preserved and perhaps slightly modified values which place so much emphasis on mutual support and the security of both the family and the new, larger social grouping of the unit. And while guanxi may make getting things done in China puzzling to an outsider, what can really be said against a system which tempers wants by forcing an approach to their eventual price in human relationships and bases commerce and power on the experience of friendship and the security of connections. For guanxi answers its own chief criticism, that recommending relatives and friends may put fools or worse in power, with the powerful fact that you will lose your own influence by doing so. Any system which fosters the security of those near to one while forcing one to a close study of their merits and suitability must finally breed honesty and compassion. In all of the complex ways that the old China preserves into the new are borne forward ancient and tried ways for human beings to interact for their mutual benefit. It is almost as if China had been preparing for the economic theories of Karl Marx, wanting only the great leveling of all men to tune its society to the modern age. If the political realities are not yet perfected, and the Chinese themselves assert that their own brand of socialism is still two hundred years from the Communist ideal, it may perhaps be because they are in the throes of complexity of continuing to save so much of the old China without tarnishing the ideals of the new.

How To Be Part Of
A Foreign "Invasion"

This was to have been a book about China, in particular about Shanghai, but even up to this point it has really been a book about what I saw, or think I saw, while I was there. And as I realize that, I realize that I must write more directly about what it is like to be a foreigner in Shanghai to give you a sense of what kind of interaction has given me my impressions. And in so doing I will still be talking about Shanghai because the interactions we had and what we felt in Shanghai will reflect the way our hosts received us and, I hope, tell you a good deal about the city. So this chapter is about us, about my family, myself and our occasional "family" of some four hundred foreign teachers in Shanghai in 1985.

A pivotal term for grasping the foreigner's situation in Shanghai is friendly misunderstanding. And for me the epitome of this state, the little model moment for a whole year of such moments, is the memory of the man who came to our door. He came to the door of our apartment with the best of goodwill and slightly excited because he had been charged with a message for us, probably. He tried to give Emma the message but her Chinese couldn't cope so he tried to give it to Susan, but her Chinese couldn't cope. He became more excited, in a friendly, enthusiastic and slightly frustrated manner. Finally a light dawned (I do not like to think what his skein of logic must have been). He whipped out a scrap of paper and a pencil, wrote down the message and proudly handed it to us. We smiled, accepted it and he left happy. There he was, confident he had delivered his message (to the deaf?). There we were, with a message we could not read and could not even interpret from the dictionary, because handwritten Chinese is even more personal and idiosyncratic than western handwriting.

This faintly ridiculous little moment is very revealing if you look at all sides of it. First, the gentleman at the door was trying to help us. Second, we tried to help him help us. Third, his best effort was no help at all. And fourth, we were embarrassed at not being any better off after his best try and we saved him the embarrassment of knowing that he had failed. We parted with mutual smiles, but nothing was achieved.

Too much of this reflects perfectly the interaction between the foreigner and his Chinese hosts. To begin with, the language difference makes it very difficult for both sides to understand each other and this can result in little comedies or more serious moments in, say, the doctor's office. There is no doubt that we should be speaking Chinese but just organizing to teach English five days a week and cope with a strange country is all most of us can manage. So our conversations with students and friends are in English and that is the first barrier.

The second barrier is that almost all the underpinnings of any human conversation depend on the unspoken question: "Where do I stand with you?" This is a particularly difficult question to answer with any stranger but it is a monumentally difficult problem to solve in a culture with such socially sophisticated signals as those we encounter in China. Besides not speaking Chinese we suffer from a lack of clues in behavior. As I have already mentioned, we were told that the great kindness shown to Japanese visitors came from the Chinese practice of being kind to those they hate. On occasions we wondered if some of the kindnesses extended to us, particularly at times when there was stress in our relationships with our hosts, were not an aspect of this method. On other occasions we were in no doubt about the motives be-

96

hind our hosts' actions but perhaps we should have been. The very first thing that hits the foreigner, if he takes only a moment to think about it, is that all of the signals; laughter, politeness, even upset are different from those at home. Even tone of voice is different in a language where words rise and fall but sentences do not. "You will go home now," which I often took for a statement bordering on an order, was in fact usually a question. The tiny slip in English grammar is compounded because the sentence would lack the rising tone of a question in English.

So how does the foreigner cope? In a word, awkwardly. In two words, awkwardly and uncertainly. The most difficult question is whether to be a "Bull in a China Shop" and go on in one's own way, or whether to worry oneself into social and professional immobility. Take the matter of cheese. In Shanghai cheese is rarely eaten, but it was available at the Foreign Food Store, a special store tucked away on a second floor on Szechuan Bei Road above a small market which supplied the foreigners' hotels. Here those of us with a special card identifying us as foreigners who were cooking for themselves (those living in hotels could not officially use the store) could buy a variety of quality foods, some of which were imported and hence had to be paid for with wai wei, the foreigners' currency. But most of their produce, once one stopped looking longingly at Rose's Lime juice and French wines and quality Scotch Whiskey, was Chinese, including excellent dry goat cheese from the North. But it ran out in September and for four months there was no cheese in Shanghai with the exception of fiercely expensive and pale tasting Kraft Velveeta imported from Kraft Australia. Then that ran out. Every day parties of foreigners visited the Foreign Food Store and asked for cheese. We got smiles and shakes of the head. No cheese. No idea when cheese would arrive. And at this point in the impasse several things come home to you. First, there is no one to raise Cain with even if you bring a Chinese speaker with you. You discover the great disconnection which operates in Chinese commerce. The store manager only gets the supplies that are delivered. The delivery man only brings what waits for him at the train station and the train only carries what has been put on it at the station near the dairy. And so on back to the sheep. So all objections and particularly violent ones are addressed to the wrong party. More importantly, the whole thing is clearly a case of mad foreigners again, because of course no one in their right mind actually *eats* cheese, do they? (Descriptions of pizza and cheese sauces notably turned the stomaches of my students when we were discussing eating habits.) And there is the problem. It is culturally ignorant to need cheese and any fuss makes one seem a fool and a boor. The alternative is to become Chinese, but while you can work at that there are leaps which are impossible to make. Our children could rarely cope with Chinese cooking and we would certainly have been in desperate straits had it not been for central heating and hot running water. So you do not become as a Chinese and you put up with a good deal of the feeling that what you need is absurd and somehow embarrassing because, although the words are unspoken, there are hints that you are making a great fuss over nothing. I got into my worst scrape in Shanghai because I shook my fist inches from a driver's face when he continued to rush into the foreign apartment compound playing his horn when children were sleeping early in the morning, after he had been repeatedly told by me by a variety of signs for several weeks and after he had been warned in Chinese several times by the wai ban at my request (and in my presence). I suspect, although his monumental stubborness was never explained to me, that in what he took to be the overall din of the city he had a driver's right to blow his horn at any time. After our confrontation I was given another driver but I am certain that in the motor pool I am still thought of as the foreign madman who assaulted a driver for absolutely no reason. Perhaps I was thought to be diseased. Or just foreign.

This difficult choice comes home for a teacher when he is constantly being reassured that he is in China to help by providing new methods and offering useful criticism of the system as it stands. And although you become doubtful of the exact meaning of "criticism" when you compare the delicate, complex and extremely sensitive natures of the Chinese people with the style of public or written self-criticism which you may hear of in Shanghai, you accept the request at face value and begin to recommend changes and improvements. Likewise you propose innovations in response to the invitation. And then you pause and wonder if you should be doing this. After all, you are a foreigner and you don't begin to understand China and Chinese ways. So, like the bull in the China shop, only uncertainly, you press forward and then you come up against "It is not our custom in China." Catch 22, Chinese style. "Please give us your ways and your methods." "It is not our custom in China."

This, I think, must be what makes China different from other Third World countries. Where they want in on the big pie of progress, China, with a history which was never really colonial and a culture whose roots disappear backward in time, is not willing to surrender its hard-won modern peace and coherence for a slice of that pie. My students and I often argued about whether it will be possible for China to get Western advantages without Western problems. While we were in Shanghai girls started wearing tweed midi-skirts, and the first event I was shepherded to after our arrival was a Western-style fashion show with Chinese models showing Chinese-made clothes which largely emulated Parisian fashion. Yet those new clothes carry with them a whole vocabulary of sexual behavior and allure in the West, and the question is whether the Chinese can put on the clothes without putting on the manners of the societies from which they come.

On a much larger scale is the question of other changes which China is making, perhaps not always with consideration of costs. When I am caught up in the Catch 22 of suggesting teaching innovations I am seeking to improve the learning of English essentially *within* the social mechanism of teaching as I have known it in Canada. Part of the difficulty of bringing my methods to bear lies in the fact that I want a more "democratic" classroom, one in which students are actively speaking and creating. But this flies in the face of ages of learning at the master's feet and in the face of the essential Chinese respect for authority. On a far vaster scale lies the question of what will come from the present Chinese efforts to "Westernize" its business and economic practices. My students made it clear to me that China is studying Western business practice so carefully in order to select from it the useful practices while fitting them into the Chinese Socialist way.

It was here that we differed and many fascinating discussions ensued as to what would happen when the systems clash. In Chinese factories there are very sharp limits to the decision-making capabilities of the leadership. There are often too many people for the requirements of the work or the available raw materials, but as the workers are all members of the same unit and are attached to it for their houses, food and other necessities, and as this is the social organization of China, workers simply cannot be let go if they are not needed. If Western practices of management were employed in industrial China social chaos would follow.

Likewise, Chinese industry does not seem to be following Western concepts of quality control but my students suggested that it has to, and soon. I had to wonder. China is still clearly a vast seller's market where everything available for domestic consumption is snatched up as quickly as it reaches the stores if it evades the guanxi, "I have a friend in the business," aspect of distribution. And as things stand buyers must look closely at every item they pick up, for many will have flaws. I had difficulty finding a 35mm slide viewer in Shanghai because Chinese photographers are keen on color print film, and when I did find a store selling them I opened and

100

examined seven viewers before buying the eighth. All seven had major flaws such as lens scratches, loose electrical connections, non-functioning bulbs and the like. While it may have been simply that I was looking for an unusual item in this case, there was no doubt about the quality control problems with items such as clothes. But here sudden improvements might bring other social disasters. In every Shanghai local market we saw literally hundreds of small tradesmen doing tailoring repairs and adjustments. One amazing craftsman specialized in replacing missing teeth in zippers and he and his mass of fellow specialists could have been impoverished if clothing quality control had suddenly improved.

Over these and many other examples my students and I ranged. "A free market economy must be free," I said, "and then people will move about to the highest paying jobs, such as the schoolteacher selling free market shirts. "No," said my students. "money will not be the sole motivation." "Oh!" I said, "but it is the sole motivation, the structural key to the Western system you say you want." "Can you," I asked over and over, "buy the technology and the methods in a box or must you accept against your will the ways of the systems you want to emulate?" And while this question can have no answer this side of history, my students assured me, as they prepared to move into roles in this shifting system and form it for the future, that China has the strength and the sense of its direction to take only what it needs to build socialism. It has certainly done so over the ages, absorbing conquerers, systems, and ideas from all those who have come to the center of the world.

Those who came to Shanghai to teach joined a wild rumor mill about what people were paid, how they were treated, whether there was cheese at the Foreign Food Store, whether Canadians could go to the American Consulate Party, whether to have shots for Japanese encephalitis, where the good restaurants were, who had tapes of *The Carpenters* (a favorite American group in China) and how to get cheap fares to San Francisco (via Hong Kong). This was abetted by the frequent and exceptionally strange occasions when they came together with the help of our hosts for a tour and party on the river, or a Christmas dancing party, or as groups of guests at International Gymnastics displays, or at the 35th anniversary fireworks party.

Many of these events offered local interpretations of what Westerners must enjoy, a mixture of ideas hung over from thirty-five years ago and the curiously filtered contemporary vision of the West. We often wondered if the events were for our hosts' entertainment, watching the foreigners on display, as much as they were for our pleasure. Yet there was always a kindness, and given the variety of nationalities and ages it would have bordered on the miraculous if entertainments to everyone's taste could have been devised. Such a varied assembly could hardly be imagined, although it seems Shanghai has a long tradition of assembling all sorts from all places. It is small wonder our hosts treated us all differently, considering how different we were to start with. Among our numbers I identified retired professors seeking a change, school teachers recruited by their professional associations, Sinophiles immersed in antiques and the classics, secret missionaries (the Christian Church has religious freedom in China but the history of missionaries has made them persona non grata), and my favorites, the "linguistic remittance men." This last group, often with families in tow, wander the world teaching a year or two here or there, using English or German as the nineteenth-century remittance man used his cheque from home to stay away from the society of his birth and wander to strange climes. One of these families that we knew came from a most quiet country in Europe, and on their teaching migration through Athens, Istanbul, Tehran (left quickly), Argentina, and Jakarta had had four children, each in a different country. They were truly without roots, seeking the new and unusual while at the same time shepherding small children to try to give them a sense of family without place. And while some of these itinerants are true adventurers they often seem to be getting by by moving on, staying just ahead of shabby reputations. One teacher we met, a gentle soul, spent his year in Shanghai reading a short story each day in his class and then chatting about it. The very indeterminacy of this sort of career, with even the longest of stays on three- or five-year contracts, probably means that host countries like China get less than fully professional foreign teachers. While it is the Chinese way, and a wonderfully warming way at that, to seek long-term friendships with its teachers and invite them to return, it is probable that only a devoted few really gifted teachers work in Shanghai at any one time. The rest of us are a motley crew, doing what we can with more goodwill than skill, having a very special experience and probably learning as much as we teach.

The heart of the "foreign invasion" of Shanghai is the lobby of the Peace Hotel, where the tourists and foreign businessmen pass through and the foreign teachers often gather to watch them interact with the hotel staff and the Chinese whom they meet. By the end of a year in Shanghai the sight of fat middle-aged ladies in halter tops and pink Bermuda shorts has ceased to be merely comic and begins to look like an insult to China, a country where women usually keep their shoulders covered. The forceful, overbearing and demanding nature of foreign tourists results in frequent contretemps, and as we have already long since discovered that you can't order a taxi any more quickly at the desk in the hotel lobby which dispenses them by shouting in any language, least of all English, we cannot really understand what those foreigners are doing arguing at the counter. In the evenings the Coffee Shop/Bar of the hotel features the world's oldest jazz band, frozen in time as a cafe orchestra in the late thirties and wheeled out nightly to play and occasionally allow a drunken tourist to get up and sing "When the Saints Go Marching In."

To the air-conditioned interior of this amazing art deco lobby, in the very hotel where Noel Coward wrote *Private*

Lives (surely the most wonderful thing ever achieved by anyone in bed for three days with a cold), we retreat for cold
Coke or Tonic Water after adventures in the tropical heat of
the Nanjing Lu. And from this lobby, often in one of the air-
conditioned taxis which made me feel slightly guilty as they
pushed arrogantly through the night carrying foreigners, we
would be returned to our flat after dinner in the exciting restaurant of the hotel, exciting often as not because unordered
dishes would arrive or be different from the previous time
they had been tried off the same menu.

The greatest charm of Shanghai is its constant variety. We
never ceased to talk to one another of the wonders and the
daily sights, exchanging not only the gossip about cheese but
the very scenes of the city itself. I got lost on my bicycle
one day and did a four-mile tour of the docks that no one
else seemed to have done. Others rose at dawn to do Tai Chi,
and I can testify to that only on their report. Still others had
tales of truly mad drivers, of gory bicycle-truck accidents,
and of the striking number of twins and triplets to be seen,
the Shanghai answer to the one-child policy. But always the
foreign "invaders" found themselves invaded by the charm,
bustle, newness, antiquity, invention, joy and energy of
Shanghai, a city which one will always go back to, in memory
if not in fact, as a part of life's experience not to be matched
or bettered.

The Energy Starts Here

Shanghai and China are changing with breathtaking speed, particularly considering the mammoth undertaking of changing so vast a country with such an immense population. In the present sweep of movement to absorb some Western ways and bring about the Four Modernizations by the end of the twentieth century, much has been written from outside China about how the course of the Communist Revolution of Mao Zedong and his comrades has been halted in favor of economic pragmatism. As a thoroughly unprofessional China watcher who asked students and friends and Chinese colleagues I think nothing could be further from the truth. I do not think there ever was *a* single course for the Revolution and the only attempt to create one, the Cultural Revolution of the mid to late 1960's, is looked back upon as the greatest deviation from the real course of events. That real course is as uncertain as any future, for the Chinese know that they wish to advance their socialism to a communism in the future, but they do not claim to know exactly how to do it. It has never been done completely anywhere else, after all, and it most certainly is unlike anything ever attempted in all of the vast history of China. But not knowing what to do exactly in the long run does nothing to quell the bursting energy of China today and particularly of Shanghai, its commercial hub. This last chapter is about the sheer energy which is the most typical feature of Shanghai, the aspect of Chinese life which leaves the deepest impression of any of the million facets of a year of wonder.

When we landed in Shanghai in an August dusk we actually had to walk through rubble after we cleared immigration because they were building a new airport under floodlights. When we left the next June it was finished, a large, gleaming modern air terminus. In the city they are building at every turn, hardly hampered by the fact that much of the work is hand labor, the moving and laying of endless streams of brick to build literally thousands of six-story apartment buildings to accommodate the growing population and to rehouse the populations of the shanty towns as they are demolished. Our area in the north of the city was thick with these new buildings, as well as new factories whose shells and inevitable surrounding walls went up completely in the year of our stay. All of the universities we saw were building furiously, and our own was opening a satellite campus on which modern buildings stood in a jumble of dirt and construction equipment, buildings already full of active learning and enthusiastic students.

In the center of Shanghai the new buildings are chiefly office blocs and hotels, although the chief new building we actually got to know at the end of our stay was the new Friendship Store, a five-story department store replacing the old, smaller three-story wooden-floored store in the role of chief salesplace to foreign visitors (and select Chinese with strong guanxi). Plans are afoot for more changes which may even defile the famous profile of buildings along the Bund, but it is difficult to imagine any real argument against the destruction of what are, after all, a series of buildings which were built by and for the interlopers who occupied the British and American Concessions for less than a century.

To the southwest of the city the Shanghai Sheraton was nearing completion next to the superb indoor Olympic pool and gymnastics center. And further south an amusement park is opening in stages, its enthusiasm and new gleam only slightly marred by the slightly twisted English names of some of the rides such as "ATMIC RIDE" and "PARAT ROOPER." And while one tunnel snakes to completion under the Huang Po, a second is planned and the proposed Shanghai subway has moved into the detailed planning stages. Shanghai, already a giant among the world's cities, has rolled up its sleeves, put on its woven bamboo hard hats, and got to work with a great will.

There are other energetic changes taking place throughout the city. On my way to teach I used to pass the licencing station where imported cars, mainly Japanese, were approved after they came off the docks. Perhaps 250 cars passed through on an average day and in the course of just one year we saw the radical upgrading of the fleet of taxis in the city and the appearance of new multiperson vans in the hands of factories and universities.

This intensity of activity does inevitably create certain temptations as everyone rushes to get some of the new vehicles. Our English language *China Daily* told of the matter of 100 Fiats, which did not exist, but which were nonetheless sold three times by middlemen in profitable paper transactions. It is hardly surprising that such activities are severely punished in a society which places such a high value on trust in all relationships, nor does it seem likely that human greed is going to be much easier to eliminate in China than anywhere else on the face of the Earth.

There was nothing imaginary about the work day in China, which starts with a 0630 hours military march over loudspeakers and people jogging or doing exercises. We quickly learned to sleep through the loudspeakers. Our students spent six or more hours a day in classes, several hours studying and often several hours on busses, yet they still found time for sports and other activities. No little part of the vitality of the city is its numerous markets, which organize before dawn and run through long days of fierce activity. Chinese housewives are often at market at 0600 hours and they average three hours a day in food preparation alone in a society where ready prepared foods are almost unheard of. If they are working as well their days are long and arduous. Yet again the energy is there.

The citizens of Shanghai and of China are doing something. While the goals of the Four Modernizations may initially sound like a propaganda campaign (perhaps because of the repeated failures of vaunted Soviet central planning) one comes to realize that the Chinese people are building their country, right now, and they know it. There is a very real sense of community and of action, not in some ideal way but fraught with all of the human imperfections of getting anything done under difficult circumstances. And with the action there is a confidence that it is getting done, a frontier spirit within one of the oldest settled civilizations on Earth. I do not know what this spirit must be like on the geographical frontiers of Chinese development, in the land reclamations from swamp and desert, but the works of fiction about it suggest a devotion, a belief and a selflessness which would inspire awe. I can see it mirrored in Shanghai; in the students, in the dockers, in the construction workers, in the teachers, in the bus drivers, in the women crew bosses in the small metal-working factory that stood near our bus stop. It is a spirit that may be lost in the West where we have, have, have, and open another beer and change the channel by remote control. In Shanghai people like their pleasures too, but they have got to get on with it, and they are getting on with it.

I have a final image out of the swirling kaleidoscope of crowds and action and kindnesses and sounds and sights and smells which I, like others charmed by the "place above the sea" (the literal meaning of Shanghai), have tried fruitlessly to capture for you. The image is from a theatre where I watched the Shanghai Ballet Company dance well in several excerpts from Western classical pieces, with one exceptional young ballerina who has already won awards in Europe and has returned in triumph to her city. Then there came a pas de deux, a new dance, which is at once Chinese and universal, original in choreography yet retaining the grace of the nineteenth century classical forms. The woman, trapped within a great ring hanging suspended from the flies, attempts to escape and is repulsed by invisible walls, nor can her lover break the bar from the outside. It is quite unlike any of the modern dance I have ever seen, a synthesis from the different perspective of coming to both modern and classical dance from the outside and blending the two without the discomforts of so-called modern choreography in classical companies or the dismissal of beauty for strangeness that so often dominates modern dance. This dance is neither. It is new, it is strange, it is Chinese, it is beautiful. In this moment of beauty that comes from the boundless effort of the young Shanghai dancers, the years of preparation and of practice, is the image of what is being built by the people of Shanghai and China who with energy and boundless spirit are facing the fearsome complexities of building their new society in their newly united land.

Epilogue

Epilogue

Books don't get written in a day or a week, so I am now writing this ending over a year after our return to Canada. Coming away from Shanghai and trying to get some perspective has been a challenge almost as great as spending the year in the city above the sea. First there was the initial impact of American style living. We took a three-week holiday in California on the way back and lived through the successive shocks of supermarkets, television, Disneyland and simply being in a world where English was almost always spoken. Then we had to set up home again and discover that everyone was asking "How was China?" and expecting us to explain a year of our lives in a truly different society in a paragraph or two. I took to the defense of saying, "It was really great," and stopping there to see if that satisfied the questioner or if he or she was intelligent or interested enough to formulate further questions.

Now we can stand back and look at our time in Shanghai and decide what to do with the experience. Today, as I finish this volume, I am ceremonially smoking the last of 100 excellent Chinese cigars I brought back and longing to be able to bicycle to the corner and buy the last good 7-cent cigars that I shall ever see. And through the cloud of lovely blue smoke, what do I see?

I see that we want to go back to China and that we are undertaking arrangements to that effect. We've not put a rosy hue of nostalgia over the difficulties of adaptation when one goes to Shanghai but these are vastly outweighed by the pleasures, excitements and the kindness of the hosts. So we are spraying out application forms and getting ready to loan out our cats in the next year or so.

But above the motivations which make one a sort of long-stay tourist is the more important idea that one is doing something to help, albeit something infinitesimally tiny in the vast mosaic of China. Our hosts certainly made sure we felt that way and, moreover, everyone around us was doing the same thing, performing small *but important* parts of "project China." For all of the problems and failures of socialist states and despite the fact that no government will ever eliminate human greed or sloth or the quirks of personalities, one of the indubitable advantages of a socialist state is the sense that we are all in this together, with each other rather than against each other. At home, here in Canada, I now read and watch and listen with a new and wry perspective to the hassles and posturings of big business, labor, special interest groups and the famous "Canadian people" (or "American people" as I watch the TV news) who everyone in public life feels suited to speak for on every issue. All these groups are fighting each other and it seems hard to imagine, competitive ethic notwithstanding, how this is good for human relationships or for that all-important sense of being valued by others. That sense was certainly accentuated in Shanghai, and not the least of our reasons for going back will be to see how and if the new, competitively-oriented economic reforms are changing the sense of pulling together in which even foreigners find themselves caught up.

Since we have returned we have not lost our contacts with China. A student from the P.R.C. studying English is living with us, so we still get the *China Daily* and we often eat his jiaozi, the delicious meat and spice filled dumplings of Shanghai (which transmute into won ton in South China, where they appear in soups). We have celebrated the Moon Festival with Chinese students at our university and we have talked with a considerable flow of people who want to know what to expect when they go to China. Needless to say it is nearly impossible to answer that for so vast and varied a country, but we offer the best advice we can. Susan is still preparing her Ph.D. on China and so the piles of books grow in our study, refreshing our memories with "Oh! That explains. . . " or "That's wrong, that's not how they do it." And one of my M.A. graduates is now teaching in Xiangtan, Hunan Province, the first of what I hope will be many people who I will advise to go.

But beyond the memories, and the future, lies what is for me the greatest value of my Shanghai year: a new baseline, a new perspective on everything that is around me. I have lived abroad before, but never in such a different place nor in a place where the people had such a sense of their own worth. There is another way: the Shanghai way. In some ways it is better, in some ways not so. But I am changed, aware of looking with new eyes at the things I used to take for granted. So, as I let the cigar die peacefully in the ashtray, I remember and I write. I hope that this little book offers some shadow of our year in Shanghai. For if it does, you will have enjoyed it.

Guelph, 1986